Praise for *Prime*

"The step-by-step guide to scho... ...rs wanted. Kids thrive in structure, a... ...t weeknight routine that helps children feel nurtured and families feel connected, all while getting things done!"

—**Kyle Schwartz, teacher and author of** *I Wish My Teacher Knew*

"Prime Time Parenting is a much needed and detailed guide for contemporary parents rearing children in a new and challenging digital society. Heather Miller provides a wealth of concrete, practical suggestions for helping parents deal with the many obstacles screen technology poses for healthy parenting."

—**David Elkind, author of** *The Hurried Child* **and** *The Power of Play*

"In a fast-paced, information-rich world, parents need to work harder than ever to provide a nurturing, predictable, and upbeat home life. Heather Miller's *Prime Time Parenting* helps parents define the best uses of technology for their growing children. This makes it an indispensable guide for the busy, modern parent."

—**Dr. Mariko Gakiya, SHINE Advisory Board member, Harvard T.H. Chan School of Public Health**

"Prime Time Parenting belongs on the bookshelf of every parent who means well and tries hard but is often so tired and stressed that the precious time we have with our families at the end of the day can unravel in chaos. Heather Miller has written a no-nonsense and supremely helpful guide designed to not only bring sanity and structure to family evenings, but to create the space to connect with the very people who give our lives so much joy and meaning."

—**Brigid Schulte, award-winning journalist, author of the New York Times best-selling** *Overwhelmed: How to Work, Love & Play When No One Has the Time*, **and director of the Better Life Lab at New America**

"No longer can parents complain that there are no owners' manuals for raising children. In *Prime Time Parenting*, Heather Miller presents an exemplary step-by-step guide to help parents make productive use of every minute during a critical and often stressful time in a family's day—6 to 8 p.m. weekdays. Based on best practices, and organized around family routines and meaningful rituals, this engaging book provides a valuable resource for any parents interested in strengthening their family's health, happiness, and well-being."

  —Ron Slaby, Ph.D., senior scientist, Center on Media and Child Health, Boston Children's Hospital

"*Prime Time Parenting* is a simply brilliant balm for the digital age. Heather Miller provides a realistic blueprint for giving your children the childhood we all crave: one where families gather around dinner tables, linger over bedtime stories, and tuck children into bed. As a parent of three boys and an expert in social and emotional learning, I think you'll find that this book helps you to regain connection with your children and enjoy valuable adult time, all while supporting healthy development for every member of the family."

  —Laura Parker Roerden, author of *Net Lessons* and executive director, Ocean Matters

Prime Time
PARENTING

Prime Time PARENTING

The Two-Hour-a-Day Secret to Raising Great Kids

Heather Miller

Da Capo
LIFE
LONG

Da Capo Press
Hachette Book Group
1290 Avenue of the Americas, New York, NY 10104
www.dacapopress.com
@DaCapoPress

Printed in the United States of America
First Edition: January 2018

Published by Da Capo Press, an imprint of Perseus Books, LLC,
a subsidiary of Hachette Book Group, Inc. The Da Capo Press name and logo
is a trademark of the Hachette Book Group.

The Hachette Speakers Bureau provides a wide range of authors for speaking events. To find out more, go to www.hachettespeakersbureau.com or call (866) 376-6591.

The publisher is not responsible for websites (or their content) that are not owned by the publisher.

Editorial production by Lori Hobkirk at the Book Factory
Print book interior design by Cynthia Young at Sagecraft

Library of Congress Cataloging-in-Publication Data has been applied for.

ISBNs: 978-0-7382-8461-3 (paperback); 978-0-7382-8462-0 (ebook)

LSC-C

10 9 8 7 6 5 4 3 2 1

This book is dedicated to two legendary educators who have helped hundreds of children and parents become the best that they can be.

Brenda Carrasquillo-Sillen

and

Joann Rossin

Contents

Preface

Parenting in the Digital Age

My working life brings me into New York City schools on a regular basis. As an expert in the teaching of reading, critical thinking, and writing, I work in a wide range of schools to improve learning outcomes in these areas. This gives me the privilege of getting to work with students as young as four and as old as eighteen, sometimes all in the same day.

Recently I walked into a sixth-grade classroom. It was the second period of the day, and a boy was fast asleep in his chair. I drummed my fingers on his desk. When he woke up I asked him if I should send out for coffee. He rubbed his eyes, blinking, still somewhere between waking and sleeping. Then, to the great amusement of his classmates, he agreed that coffee would be a great idea. I smilingly pointed out that I could not get him a coffee because he was only eleven years old, and here we were at school at ten in the morning. The rest of the class found our little exchange highly amusing, and as an isolated incident, I did too.

But it's not an isolated incident. Throughout the last several years at schools in widely different neighborhoods, I've seen young children who are clearly suffering from sleep deprivation. Through conversations with these students, I've learned some of the reasons for their fatigue:

Some stay up late doing homework.

Some have flexible bedtimes and end up getting much less sleep than the recommended nine to eleven hours.

Some play video games late into the night with or without their parents' permission.

Some, after their parents put them to bed, continue to play digital games on their phone, tablet, or other device—or engage with social media deep into the night.

We might expect some of these scenarios in teens, but we're increasingly seeing them in elementary and middle school children. The digital age has changed how we live—and how our children live. Adults have a responsibility to wisely integrate technology into our children's lives. That includes carving out significant time each day for screen-free time, opportunities for quiet activities, and face-to-face conversation. Establishing a balance for our children encourages the development of the whole child. However, we can't give what we don't have. Parents need to establish healthy screen habits in order for their children to enjoy the same.

Most adults have learned to navigate the subtleties of the digital world. We've figured out that a Facebook friend is not the same thing as a friend you roomed with in college. We know that the amazing affordances of Skype and teleconferencing aren't perfect substitutes for communication with people who are physically present. And we are increasingly aware that our tendency to be tethered to our smartphones damages our closest relationships.

The average American parent spends more than seven hours a day in front of screens *for personal use.** When combined with screen use for work, that amounts to more than nine hours each day. As most of us will freely admit, our concentration spans, our sleep habits, and even our conversational skills are negatively affected by over-reliance on interactive technology.

So limiting screen time is a family-wide challenge and requires a family-wide solution.

That's just what this book is designed to offer. *Prime-Time Parenting* outlines an evening plan to help parents navigate childrearing and parental self-care in the digital age. Informed by the latest research in child development and cognitive science as well as ancient wisdom on what works best for children, it outlines a two-hour routine that covers the bases of homework, family dinner, reading, bath time, and bedtime. Importantly, it leaves plenty of time for the parent to relax, refresh, and recharge themselves.

Why devote a book entirely to school nights? As challenging as school nights are to tired parents, they are critical to the development of school-age children. Reconnecting with family; processing the events of the day; facing down the challenges of homework and nightly reading; receiving nourishment in the form of healthy food, parental attention and lively conversation; and falling asleep at a reasonable time—all of these habits set the child up for success the following morning. Over time, they teach a child how to care for himself as well as how to care about others too.

---

* Parents here are those with children aged eight to eighteen.

While the structure outlined in *Prime-Time Parenting* excludes screen media between 6:00 p.m. and 8:00 p.m., I should make clear that I am an avid fan of digital technology. In fact, I've worked on cutting-edge educational technology projects throughout my career and have earned graduate degrees from MIT and Harvard Graduate School of Education, both leaders in the study and development of new educational tools. But after more than two decades of immersion in digital media, I simply believe that the best users of any form of technology know when to use it and when to switch it off.

That's a lot easier said than done, especially where children are concerned. The prospect of cutting a child off from a social media app or video game can feel a lot like depriving them of oxygen. The ensuing temper tantrums and irritability are sure signs that children are spending too much time in front of screens. And if that doesn't convince you, a look at the data lays bare the facts.

In 2018 the average American child spent six to seven hours on digital media a day. The effects of all that screen time can include decreased powers of concentration, increased stress levels, difficulty controlling mood and behavior, poor eye contact, and low frustration tolerance. And that's before we get into what all those hours in front of screens *displaces*. After all, if a child is spending six to seven hours in front of a screen, here's what she's not doing: playing with friends, drawing, building, reading, making things, working on puzzles, talking to family members, participating in sports, developing extracurricular hobbies and skills, completing school work, helping out with chores, and sleeping. Our children's ability to develop into thoughtful, creative, and curious people depends on significant daily time engaged in worthwhile, screen-free activities. When screen time nudges these aside, a child's social, emotional, and intellectual development is compromised.

Tellingly, some of the very people who have created the technology that floods our lives set strict limits on their own children's use of it. Bill Gates has stated, "We often set a time after which there is no screen time, and in their case that helps them get to sleep at a reasonable hour." When asked what his children thought of the iPad, Steve Jobs famously replied in 2010, "They haven't used it. We limit how much technology our kids use at home." Hearing this, I was stunned. At the time I was consulting in inner-city public schools, which were making massive investments in iPads. These schools saw it as a bid to traverse the "digital divide." I remember a principal proudly telling me that each and every child in her school would have their own tablet. That represented an investment of hundreds of thousands of dollars for a single school. And yet its creator had not let his own children use it. Clearly there was a disconnect between what educators and technology leaders perceive as important in twenty-first-century education. Today a surprising number of Silicon Valley executives send their children to technology-free Waldorf schools, where hands-on learning and physical activity are emphasized. Many schools in the Waldorf tradition not only ban technology from the classroom; they also discourage children's use of it at home.

That reluctance to let children use much—or even any— screen media may be informed by an understanding of just how addictive they can be. Pierre Laurent, a former Microsoft marketing manager and parent, explained, "Media products are designed to keep people's attention. It's not that there's an intent to harm children, but there's an intent to keep them engaged." It's no accident that children don't want to get off their devices; these applications and games were designed to be "sticky."

In contrast, when children read, write, draw, build, or play, they are learning self-control, how to focus, how to solve problems, and how to think out of the box. I saw this in my own child who grew up without a television until the age of nine. When I took him to grade school his teachers commented on his unusually well-developed reading and creative problem-solving skills. I wish I could take credit for this, but the truth is that what I did not do was every bit as important as what I did. By removing a television from our home, Jasper was forced to find ways to entertain himself, and these involved far more creativity and concentration than watching television requires.

When we watch our children engage with interactive media, we cannot deny that they look focused. However, what we are observing is computer-enabled attention, a fundamentally different quality of attention than when a person reads, builds, or writes. Computer-enabled attention may undermine a child's ability to develop real attentional control, the kind required to read and write in academic contexts. One technology executive observed that there is no harm in delaying children's engagement with technology; after all, children and teens pick up technological skills with extreme ease. What children do not pick up easily is strong reading, writing, and mathematical skills. Even "gifted" children put in enormous amounts of time to develop their skills in these areas. In fact, acquiring these foundational academic skills is so time intensive that most children need to work at it during the school day and again at home during homework. It takes years and years of concerted, nearly daily practice to produce a college-ready reader and writer. When we underestimate just how much time mastery in these areas require, our children pay for it with reduced prospects.

So *Prime-Time Parenting* includes enjoyable practices that help children lengthen their attention span and strengthen their literacy and numeracy skills. It also offers tips and techniques for helping children organize their homework and school bags and prepare for the coming day. This will help them arrive at school the next morning feeling relaxed, prepared, and confident.

What is a teacher's dream? A child who follows a regular routine, such as the one outlined in this book, on school nights. Why? Because that child has completed and organized their assignments, practiced or deepened the skills learned the previous day, read independently and together with a parent, had a nutritious meal, enjoyed rich conversations with family, and had a good night's rest. That is a perfect recipe for a student who arrives each morning bright eyed and bushy tailed, ready, willing, and able to learn.

Teachers, parents, and students are partners. They each have a unique role to play. If any one of the three falls down on the job, educational progress won't happen. At this point in our nation's educational history there are wide spectrums of opinion about the usefulness of homework or the fairness of state exams or the wisdom of the Common Core standards. Wherever you fall on these debates, I hope you work closely with your child's teacher, gaining clarity on what he or she expects from parents and fulfilling your important role in the educational mission. And if you find yourself with a teacher who strikes you as rather undemanding or hazy about just what parents should do to encourage their child's academic growth, take note that you may need to do more heavy lifting with your child's education this year than normal. *Prime-Time Parenting* and its various segments covers what even the most exacting teacher would expect from a student aged thirteen or younger.

I've worked with many schools and have seen everything from schools that expect several hours of homework at middle school, to schools where homework was assigned without any expectation of it being completed, to schools where it was not assigned at all because the school believed that students needed time to relax in the evening. And I am aware of schools that have taken a "no homework" position because they believe that children are better served in self-chosen after-school activities. I am unapologetically pro-homework. Students need the independent practice that it offers, the self-discipline and organization that it engenders, and the chance to extend work in ways not possible within the school day. Homework should be interesting, challenging, and relevant to the overarching goals of the curriculum. Even skill drills designed to build automaticity can be made interesting and designed to involve higher-order thinking. If your child's school does not assign homework at all or assigns homework that is inadequate in terms of challenge, I would strongly suggest that you assemble a homework program of your own to supplement it. (See the Resource section for more specific suggestions.)

The time you spend during the Homework Hustle segment of the evening is especially important to your child's attitude about school. By devoting that time, you are sending a clear message to your child about how important schoolwork is—and, at times, how difficult. Sitting with a child and ensuring that they are staying on task and encouraging them as they struggle with a difficult assignment tells the child that it is natural and normal to have to work hard, even when you don't feel like it and even when you don't quite know what you are doing. Over time and perhaps counterintuitively, this enables children to become self-reliant. They don't shy away from challenge, and they know better than to quit just because they're bored.

The parental role in homework that I've described in the Homework Hustle section of the book also communicates parental expectations about education. Not surprisingly, parents who express high expectations for their children's academic achievement—and follow through with warm support and firm structure—do much better than students whose parents take a more casual approach. As we all know, children learn from what parents do more than from what they say. And when parents commit themselves to ensuring that homework is done and correctly put away, their children understand that the responsibilities of schoolwork are very serious ones.

Contrast that message with a parent who believes that their child is entirely responsible for completing their homework and putting it away. The parent may believe themselves to be encouraging their child's self-reliance. In fact, they are sending a rather wishy-washy message about homework's importance—and the importance of fulfilling one's responsibilities. The parent who takes the stance that children should opt out of homework altogether on the grounds that it is worthless has now provided a very confusing message to their child, one where the teacher and the school are misguided. That sets a very difficult context for the child to succeed and grow within. Children need to "buy in" *before* they can lean in—and they are unlikely to do either if they don't see their parents doing the same.

One of the most notable attitudes in classrooms today—at every educational level—is an inability to rise to a challenge or grapple with an unfamiliar task. Many students simply do not have the patience to buckle down and work something out on their own. This lack of tolerance for difficulty shows that they haven't had to problem solve on their own enough. I see this in elementary school students all the way through to college students. What will happen to these students when they go on to professions? The ability to learn, to self-teach, and to adapt is absolutely critical in the fast-moving Information Age.

Students need to be able to sit quietly with a problem and struggle through it on their own. A child who is actively trying to produce something she has never done before, whether it's a solution to an algebra question or a new type of essay, is a child who is learning. If it is difficult for them, that's a good thing! When they conquer the challenge, they will have acquired so much more than the target skill: they will have the self-knowledge that they can tackle new and even harder challenges in time to come.

My hope is that this book provides some new ideas and inspiration for the night shift of parenting, the most challenging job of all, no matter what age we live in.

Heather Miller
New York, New York

Introduction

Prime-Time Parenting at a Glance

If you're like most parents, 6:00 p.m. isn't the end of the day—it's the start of your second shift. Whether you work in the home or outside of it, 6:00 p.m. finds you tired, zapped out, and ready to put your feet up. Unfortunately, just as your energy flags, a series of parenting tasks lie in wait:

- Preparing dinner

- Having dinner

- Checking your kids' homework

- Getting your kids through bath time

- Reading with your children

- Putting your kids to bed

How do we do it all? The answer is: too often, we *don't*.

We order dinner online or pick it up on the way home. The kids turn up at the dinner table with their eyes glued to their phones or tablets, and although you ask them to turn them off, you yourself sneak looks at your phone between mouthfuls. Dinner conversation? It's a staccato blend of one-word answers, nagging about turning the devices off, and silent pauses while everyone reads their screens.

After dinner the kids sulkily depart to do homework. At least, that's what you *hope* they're doing as you throw away the trash that contained your dinner. Then it's nag time. Nagging about homework. Nagging about bedtime. Looking over their shoulders at computer screens that ostensibly are being used for academic tasks. And prying them away from their devices. By the time the kids are more or less in bed, it's your bedtime too.

This unfulfilling cycle of nagging and negotiating turns what should be the happiest time of the day into a grueling grind. It doesn't have to be that way. The answer is what I call *Prime-Time Parenting*: a two-hour window that is going to change your life.

If we think of the two hours between 6:00 p.m. and 8:00 p.m. as our "prime-time parenting" hours, we can focus our energy on the critical parenting tasks of dinner, homework, reading, and bedtime. And then we can punch our card. We can clock out. We can claim our adult right to peace and quiet for an hour or two before we go to bed. And what are our kids doing during the adult time we have claimed for ourselves? They're doing what children are *supposed* to be doing after 8:30 p.m. They're sleeping.

Bedtime at 8 or 8:30? Even for middle schoolers?

Yes, you read that right. Children need enormous amounts of sleep. It's a fact we have largely forgotten over the last several decades. According to the American Academy of Sleep Medicine, a child between the ages of six and twelve needs nine to twelve hours of sleep each night. With adequate sleep, children enjoy better concentration, stronger memory, improved emotional regulation, and overall physical and mental health.

But my child is different! you say. He doesn't need that much sleep!

Many parents think that because a child does not appear sleepy at 8:00 p.m. that it's okay to let the child stay up later. And some parents—and even some parenting gurus—claim that "sleep anxiety" is caused by insisting a wide-awake child go to bed.

But a child who seems energetic and alert at 8:30 p.m. needs sleep just as much as a child who is visibly cranky from fatigue. Moreover, if your adorable night owl doesn't get the recommended hours of sleep tonight, he will probably be making up for it during tomorrow's math class. All children need sleep and lots of it. With a structured bedtime routine that includes a warm bath, a nice conversation with mom or dad, a little reading together, and a proper tucking in, even the most rambunctious child or energized tween will begin to power down.

The bottom line: while there are individual differences between how much sleep a person needs, *all* children need a lot of sleep. Don't let your child's charm or energy—or even your desire to have more face time with him or her—convince you otherwise.

Screen Time Interferes with Dreamtime

There's a good reason why so many of our children appear wide-awake at bedtime, and it's in front of our noses. Or, more accurately, *their* noses.

As children spend more and more time in front of screens, more and more children are having difficulty falling asleep. And the same is true of adults. The reason is biochemical. When our children interact with screens, they are exposed to the blue light that most of these devices emit.

The blue light from screens tricks our body into thinking that it is still daytime. And, in turn, our body does not release the hormone melatonin, which tells our bodies to go to sleep. This is why your nine-year-old may be super-alert at 10:00 p.m. If she's been gaming or working on a computer or even reading off of a tablet, that blue light has convinced her brain and body that it's the middle of the day, not the end of it.

Try going to sleep immediately after several hours of screen time. If you're like most people, you will have some difficulty. The blue light has thrown your body clock out of sync with the natural world. The solution: shut down the screens two hours before bedtime.

Sleep and School Performance

One of the reasons I wrote this book is because I can see the effects of lack of sleep on a day-to-day basis in schools. As a consultant to schools on improving learning outcomes for children, I get to visit many different schools and observe children in the process of classroom instruction. In recent years I have noticed an increase in children who are visibly drowsy, not just in the afternoon or immediately after lunch, but in the mid-morning. I don't remember the same fatigue in students of the same age, even just five years ago.

"You're ten years old!" I sometimes chide them. "You should have plenty of energy at 10:00 a.m. You should be raring to go!" One time recently a young girl responded, "But Ms. Miller, isn't it normal to be tired? I mean, just because we're kids, does that really mean that we should never be tired?"

I looked at the young girl for a moment. I thought about what her comment revealed. Her experience had told her that it was perfectly normal to be drowsy as a ten-year-old at 10:00 a.m.

I told her, "Of course you should feel tired sometimes. But not at ten in the morning. It's not as though you've been work-ing in the fields since 5:00 a.m. By now you've been up only a few hours. You should be wide eyed and refreshed."

Drowsy children are increasingly the rule in class, but there are also some students who are just flat-out asleep. And I'm not talking about half-asleep—I'm talking deep REM sleep. And while these children are often taking med-ication for ADHD, it is possible that a mixture of sleep deprivation *and* the effects of medication are combining to produce this deep, midmorning slumber. Either way, cer-tain students are downright unconscious when their teacher is explaining fractions or the causes of the French Revolu-tion. Why? Because their bodies are desperately trying to make up for the sleep they lost the night before. Teachers are put in the agonizing position over and over again of having to wake up a young child who is fast asleep. To my eyes it feels torturous for the child and deeply unfair to the teacher.

Fortunately, there is an easy fix for this. The Prime-Time Parenting method ensures that your children really *are* getting enough hours of sleep and are not interacting with screens in the last hour before bed. As a result, they can *feel* as tired as they actually are.

Prime-Time Parenting keeps kids (and parents) busy for the two-hour lead-up before bedtime. There is no window for screen time here. This ensures that your children's natural sleep process will occur without interference from melatonin-lowering blue light from screens. Moreover, your child will get into a more peaceful state of mind, knowing that homework is complete, the backpack is packed and ready for tomorrow morning, and they have had some high-quality time with their favorite person—*you*.

If you don't get home until after 6:00 p.m., you can still do Prime-Time Parenting. You might shift the start of Prime-Time Parenting to 6:30 or have a caregiver follow the routine until you get home.

Lessons from Long Ago

A few generations ago parents didn't have the science to support basic wisdom about parenting, such as children's need for active play time, affection, physical activity, good nutrition, many friends, predictable routines, and appropriate challenge.

Nevertheless, most parents knew what their children needed from common sense. In today's world, awash with new technologies that have rapidly changed how we communicate, play, work, interact, and record our experience, we may temporarily lose track of age-old best practices in the raising of children. And it doesn't make it any easier that we are largely unaware of the biochemical changes that extended screen time can have on our children's behavior. We can and should take a step back now, reflect on the role of screen media in our family's lives and create habits that reflect our hopes and dreams for our children, as well as our priorities for ourselves, as adults. This book helps parents identify an approach to parenting that integrates the best of new insights into child development with ancient wisdom about child-rearing.

The exclusive focus on active parenting for two hours each evening enables parents to:

- pay attention to each of their children

- ensure homework is complete

- support their child's organizational skills

- nourish their child with healthy food

- have rich conversations with their child

- support good social skills and manners

- play with their child

- read with their child

- respond to messages from school

- foster healthy sleep habits in their child

- provide a bedtime ritual that includes bath time, conversation and reading

And . . .

- *ensure well-deserved rest and relaxation for the parent*

That is a long list of achievements for an investment of just two hours. And it leaves parents with the time they need to nurture themselves and each other.

My hope is that the Prime-Time Parenting routine will help transform the evening grind into what it should be: the best part of your day.

"And what are kids doing during the adult time we have claimed for ourselves? They're doing what children are *supposed* to be doing after 8:30 p.m. They're sleeping."

YOU'RE GOING TO:

- ☑ *Check in with your children*
- ☑ *Get the kids started with homework*
- ☑ *Cook dinner*

Chapter 1

6:00 to 6:30 PM:
Prime-Time Parenting Begins

Whether you've been at home with the children for hours or just walked through the door, start Prime-Time Parenting off right by greeting your kids with what I like to call the "huddle." After all, this is the start of your evening time together. So give each of them a proper greeting and ask for one back. It may sound surprising, but greetings in general, including greetings between children and parents, are on the decline. Making a ritual of greeting your children is the best way to start each evening. The act of receiving and giving a greeting is also an important part of your child's social education. If you greet your children and insist that they greet you back, your children will be more likely to show this courtesy to others. And while you're greeting the kids, give them a hug. Aside from the obvious love it shows, hugs benefit both parent and child in a range of important and surprising ways.

Parental warmth has an enormously positive effect on children's social and emotional development. The warmer and more affectionate the parent, the more likely the child will have positive social skills. Moreover, parental warmth promotes better problem-solving skills. As individuals with a range of temperaments, some of us are naturally "warmer" than others, but we are all capable of hugging our children. So hug it out at the start of an evening. The overwhelming likelihood is that your kids need a hug—and so do you.

You may be hugging your kids less often than you realize. As our children enter grade school, we tend to hug them less frenquently than we did when they were preschoolers. More than 90 percent of moms and dads hug their three-year-olds on a daily basis, but just 50 percent of dads hug their ten- to twelve-year-olds once a day, and 26 percent of moms don't hug their ten- to twelve-year-olds on a daily basis. All children and all adults benefit greatly from daily hugs.

Benefits of Hugs

One: A hug lowers stress and strengthens our immune system. That's because hugs discourage the excessive production of the stress hormone cortisol. As a result, we avoid the negative impacts of excess cortisol: a weak immune system and inflammation.

Two: Hugging promotes the release of oxytocin, a hormone that encourages attachment in relationships. Oxytocin helps us bond to others; it also lifts moods, calms behavior, and relaxes the nervous system.

Three: Think of what a hug is: we wrap our arms around our child in a loving, protective embrace. This is the physical manifestation of parental love: warmth, nurturing, safety, and security. As important as words are, actions speak even louder. A hug is an unambiguous expression of acceptance and love. No wonder hugs have so many positive effects on human beings.

The Five-Minute Check-In

After greeting and hugging your child, take a full five minutes to check in with them. Sit down and give them a chance to tell you about their day.

Some children will jump right in and tell you everything; other children will give you one-word answers. To help these more reticent kids, ask specific questions, such as:

- What was the best part of your day?

- What was the worst part of your day?

- How did that math test go?

- Did you play with Peter at recess?

The goal here is to give your kids an opportunity to tell you how their day went and communicate anything that they want to share. This allows you to respond to their mood and give them the attention they need. At the same time, this is just a five-minute check-in. If a child feels inspired to tell you a long story, you can say, "I can hardly wait to hear the whole story, but let's save it for dinner. That sounds like a dinnertime story."

Divide and Conquer

Now that you've heard about their day, it's time to segue to the pre-dinner plan. First, it's time for the big reveal about what you've decided to make for dinner. This will give them something to look forward to as they face down the next half hour or so of homework. Then, look at your watch and say, "Well, it's about thirty minutes before dinner. Let's take a look at your assignment book and get homework started before we have a delicious meal."

Getting Kids Set Up with Homework

With a brief but meaningful check-in under your belt, it's time to get down to the big challenge: the homework part of the evening is about to begin. You might like to start this part of the proceedings a bit like a boardroom meeting. Have the children sit around the dining table. You can even ring a bell to call the meeting to order. Most children delight in this sort of formality and theatricality.

Have the kids take out their homework materials and put them on the table in front of them. It's time for them to break out the assignment notebooks and relay to you what they need to get done. Not only does this help them develop organizational skills, but it also gives them a motivational boost as they face down the dreaded tasks of school assignments. With your children seated around you at the table with their assignment books and other materials in front of them, ask, "What's on the docket for this evening?"

Go around and have each child read out their assignments. Ask them to show you the books or worksheets involved. Talk through what needs to get done. The goal is to find out if your child has everything he needs to do the homework and understands what needs to be done. This will save problems later.

Doing this gives your child a very "grown-up" feeling that you take their work seriously—and that you don't underestimate the stamina or skill required to complete it all. It also helps the child mentally rehearse what she is about to do. That makes it much, much easier for them to actually do it—and spares them from freezing up at the prospect of starting.

As parents, we can't to do our kids' homework for them, but we can and should them up for success in getting it done well. And that's why it's important to review their assignments with them and help them get organized *before* they start completing their work.

Homework Plan of Attack

Once your child has read aloud all her assignments, ask her to put the assignments in the order in which she thinks she should do them. Then ask her which one she has chosen to do first and why.

Good reasons for doing one piece of homework first might include:

- It's easy, so I can get it done fast.

- I enjoy it.

- It's due tomorrow.

- It's hard, and I want to get it over and done with.

There is no best answer here. Just asking the question "Why do you want to do that first?" builds metacognitive awareness about work preferences and strategy. The more intentional a child can become about how they organize their work, the better they will be able to focus on it.

When each child has established his "homework attack" strategy, it's time for a materials check.

Ask your kids the questions below. After each question, pause while they organize the items they need.

- Are all the homework materials—textbooks, lined paper, worksheets—on the table?

- Do we have enough pencils? Are the pencils sharpened?

- Are any other materials—such as markers, highlighters, and erasers—on the table?

With all the materials in order, their homework assignments neatly lined up, and a plan of action in place, the kids are in the ideal frame of mind to hit the books.

Use a Timer

Timers are an excellent tool for developing concentration. Most people struggle to focus in the initial stages of a task, and children are no exception. Setting a timer for a minute or two and challenging a child to work nonstop until the timer goes off can add a bit of motivation and drama to an otherwise tedious task.

Once your child has become accustomed to using a timer, incorporate it into your nightly homework routine by setting a timer for five minute intervals. Their task? To see how much they can get done in five minutes without sacrificing quality. Your child may start out by rushing, but soon something else will happen: she'll start to concentrate. And she'll discover just how much she can achieve, and what interesting thoughts occur to her, when she concentrates fully. Being fully immersed in a task is a highly pleasurable experience. Once your child gets a taste of how good it feels to "lock in" to a task, he will begin to look forward to silent homework "sprints."

As children mature and homework increases, using timers to boost concentration and productivity will prove greatly beneficial to managing larger workloads. The length of time they can concentrate naturally expands with age. As their parent, you might try using a timer at work to make the best use of your time as well.

Silent Sprints

It's not an accident that standardized exams are given in conditions of silence. Working in silence is the optimal mode for deep concentration. Don't believe anyone who tells you that having background noise is somehow a facilitator of work—it isn't. We only have so much attention; when we play music or talk while working, we divert some of our attention span to those tasks, leaving less attention available to the work at hand. As a result, we do our work less well and it takes longer.

Most of our children live in noisy environments at school, after school, and at home. Giving them some precious silent time helps them to develop a tolerance for working without these environmental stimuli. It can help them achieve at levels they might not otherwise reach. Of course, no one is suggesting that you keep the environment pin-drop silent for hours at a time; silence with young children works best in short increments. I call this "silent sprints." Depending on your child's attention span and tolerance for working independently, "silent sprints" can last anywhere from sixty seconds to fifteen minutes.

Silent sprints punctuated with visits from you every few minutes should create an ideal situation for focused homework completion. And while the kids hit the books, it's time for *you* to hit the kitchen.

See and Be Seen

You've set the timer for five minutes—or longer if your kids can handle it. Now you can go into the kitchen and get busy with dinner.

When the timer goes off, pause to check on the kids' progress. Praise their effort. Ask them how long they want the timer set this time: Can they stretch to six minutes or even seven minutes? Keep them focused by asking what they think they can get done between now and when the timer goes off again.

Most kids—like most adults—can't stay focused forever. In fact, many of us have trouble focusing at all. Your children should take justifiable pride as their ability to concentrate lengthens. And they should start noticing something else that ought to incentivize them: now that they're working in silence—and with the urgency of a timer—they're probably getting their homework done much faster.

With the youngsters motivated and focused, head back to the kitchen and cook . . . until the timer goes off again. Repeat this process until dinner is ready.

A "No Excuses" Approach

Because you've had your conversational check-in and ensured that your children are clear about their assignments and have all the materials they need, your kids are ready and able to do their homework. They may not, however, be willing. Children, just like grown-ups, exercise extraordinary creativity in getting out of work. Your job is to insist they get down to it. So unless your child has a medical condition that requires constant snacks, water, and bathroom breaks, take a hard—or at least bemused—line with the following stall tactics. They have felled many less streetwise parents in the past!

Common Stall Tactics of Avoidant Students

THE STALL TACTIC	THE PRIME TIME PARENTING RESPONSE
A sudden snack attack	Dinner is almost ready. Just think how delicious it will be with a good appetite!
A thirst that must be quenched at once if life is to be sustained	Unless your child has a medical condition that causes extreme thirst, do not feel the need to involve beverages (including water) in homework time. Children are working for short periods of time, and beverages inevitably lead to two other stall techniques: the spilled substance and the bathroom break.
The spilled substance	There shouldn't be substances on the homework table that can be spilled. But if there are spills, set a rule that they call you at once, and you swiftly clean it up. Problem solved.

Common Stall Tactics of Avoidant Students

THE STALL TACTIC	THE PRIME TIME PARENTING RESPONSE
The bathroom break	Nobody's saying you should risk an accident, but bathroom breaks should take place in the transition to Prime-Time Parenting. If this is a repeated ploy, emphasize the preemptive bathroom break during the pre-Prime-Time stage.
Amnesia about just what the homework is or how to do it	By going over the homework during Divide and Conquer, the kids should know what their homework entails. If they're really unclear, they can call a friend after dinner and work on something else until then.
A never-ending need for pencil sharpening	The materials check should have this covered. Kids need several pencils sharpened and ready to go in order to get around this tried and true stall tactic.

Also, look out for these stock characters who may appear in your home during homework time:

The Picasso of erasers. This little creature has figured out that erasing looks a lot like working. So he erases, and then erases, and then erases some more. Five minutes later he's still erasing the letter he wrote ten minutes ago. Under the guise of perfectionism—"I want to make it look neat!"—he avoids doing any actual work for as long as he can get away with it.

The storyteller. This charmer understands the power of a good story—and uses it to get out of doing her homework. How can you cut off your beloved child while she regales you with an event from her day at school? Well, you *can* and you *must*—or at least tell her to save it for dinnertime, the appropriate venue.

The fight finder. This child has figured out how to milk conflict in order to distract himself and everyone else from the fact that he is not getting his work done. First, he orchestrates the conflict. Then, he escalates the conflict. Once you intervene and solve the conflict, there is still the matter of the time-consuming emotional aftermath—his. All of this eats up homework time. Call his bluff and show no mercy.

The child bursting with affection. Who can turn down a hug from a beloved son or daughter? Well, it turns out that during homework time *you* can and should. This cynical youngster has figured out that running into the kitchen with arms extended and throwing them around you in an impromptu hug will elicit parental affection sure to eat up at least three minutes of homework time. Don't fall for it. Point out that the best way for her to show her love for you is to do her homework.

Structure Supports Brain Development

Kidding aside, a strong, predictable structure at home is like a multivitamin to your child's growing brain. It helps the brain grow in myriad positive ways.

A reliable structure with a no-nonsense approach to task completion is particularly beneficial to your child's executive function. The executive function refers to the processes in the brain that enable us to plan, focus, and follow instructions. Without executive function, it's hard for a child to filter out distractions, prioritize tasks, set and achieve goals. and control impulses. In other words, without executive function, it's very difficult to learn.

And here's something all parents should know about executive function: it's a potential, not an inherent, ability. Executive function does not develop on its own. Rather it develops in response to parenting and child-rearing practices. In homes where there is a fair bit of structure, children *seem* to develop the ability to plan and carry out complex tasks quite naturally. In fact, they have learned these skills from the structure of the home. In contrast, in homes where there is little structure and/or high stress, many children do not develop the ability to control their impulses and attention or the ability to plan and execute tasks with serious consequences for their social and academic progress.

When you implement a structure like Prime-Time Parenting, you are supporting the development of your child's brain architecture. Over time your child will be able to take on more and more complex tasks and complete them with focus, self-knowledge, and organization. This extraordinary capacity is built little by little, day after day, month after month. That's why parental consistency is so critical.

Get Cooking

You may ask yourself: *Can I cook a delicious, healthy dinner using mostly whole, nonprocessed foods in twenty to twenty-five minutes flat . . . while still being a mindful, attentive parent?* The answer to both questions is *yes*. This chapter reveals how. The meal you're going to prepare is quick, nutritious, and easy. You'll be checking in on the kids every few minutes while you cook. The kids have a built-in incentive to let you get on with it because they're hungry for dinner and eager for a homework break.

People come to cooking from many different places. Some people love to cook. Some people feel intimidated by it. If you're an experienced home cook, then you probably have your go-to meals down. You probably also know that cooking a meal with fresh ingredients is one of the best ways to relax at the end of the day. If you're a new or reluctant cook, you may need some convincing and pointers. So here they are.

Identify your fab five. Create a list of five meals that are nutritious, easy to prepare, and that your family enjoys. Nobody said that as a home cook you need to master Julia Child's entire repertoire. Instead, start out with mastering just five simple and nutritious meals. Build the meal around a good source of protein. If you're stuck for inspiration, think in terms of a fish night, a chicken night, a legume night, a pasta and salad night, and a meat night. Vegetarians will want to build their meals around good sources of protein for growing children such as lentils, chickpeas, tofu, black beans, and, if you eat them, eggs. By all means, invite your children to help identify the family's fab five.

Include vegetables in every meal. Make sure each of your fab five meals include at least two vegetables. Vegetables are the mainstay of healthy eating. So if one of your fab five is macaroni and cheese, make sure that you add a salad or a side of broccoli or sprinkle in peas and other small or cut vegetables into the macaroni and cheese itself. Get the kids involved in brainstorming how to incorporate vegetables into any meals that need more of them. Encourage children to geek out on the vitamins each vegetable offers.

Create a grocery list. Once you have your fab five meals down, create a master list of ingredients for them. Keep this list in your wallet or on a food shopping app, and take a photo of it so you can access it from your phone any time you need it.

Shop for the week. Once a week go to the grocery store to buy the ingredients you need. Healthy food is made with ingredients as close to their natural state as possible. The fewer processed and packaged foods we use and the more organic ingredients we can afford, the healthier the meal is likely to be.

A cook is only as good as the materials he works with, so choose the freshest high-quality produce you can afford.

Cook as the mood strikes you. Now that you have your ingredients for the week ahead, you can cook the dinners in whatever order strikes you as best. This is one of the great pleasures of cooking. You'll find yourself on the commute home deciding whether you want to make chicken with lemon, broccoli and brown rice, or that tofu stir-fry with red peppers and snow peas. It's the prerogative of the chef to prepare the meal that best fits his or her mood and energy level.

Have fun and try new things. As time goes on, you'll probably be inspired to expand your repertoire, try new things, adapt menus to the seasons, and move meals in and out of the fab five list. You'll find that cooking becomes a part of your imaginative life and not just a dreaded chore. You may also find, as most cooks do, that the act of cooking makes us more present, more relaxed, and just plain happier.

Cooking Solo

If you're a single parent or if your spouse or partner can't get home from work on time to cook with you, then cooking is a solo activity. Make it pleasurable by changing into comfortable clothes and playing some light music—just take care that the music isn't loud enough to distract the kids. If you enjoy a glass of wine with dinner, you can sip as you cook. You might be tempted to get on the phone while you cook, but it's best to resist that urge. For one thing, you'll want to be checking in on the kids' progress every few minutes. For another, Prime-Time Parenting is family time and, for that reason, device-free.

Cooking as a Couple

If you and your partner are lucky enough to both be home in time to cook together, then make meal preparation something you do together. As you cook, you can catch up on the day, including those bits of news that may not be appropriate for the kids to hear about.

It would be a missed opportunity to delegate the cooking task to one parent while another parent sits with the kids as they do homework—or does something else. A key tension in most marriages is the uneven distribution of household tasks.

When a couple cooks together, they are sharing the work of the marriage and the family—while also, hopefully, enjoying the chance to chat, flirt, and laugh together. It's also great for your kids to see you happily collaborating on the evening meal.

Making It Even Easier and Healthier

Use a rice cooker. Rice cookers are one of the cheapest appliances to purchase—and they are worth their weight in gold. Most come with a steamer tray that allows you to steam vegetables, fish, chicken, or tofu. You can even add a sliver of lemon or other fruit to the steamer to add flavor to the rice and the foods being steamed. It takes no more than ninety seconds to fill the rice cooker with water and brown, basmati, or jasmine rice and then place vegetables and other ingredients on the steamer tray. Then, after switching it on, you can walk away and let the rice cooker do the rest. Within minutes the fragrant scent of rice and steamed vegetables fills the kitchen. In about twenty minutes you'll have a delicious and extremely healthy meal. To add flavor, you might finish cooking the chicken or tofu in a pan for a minute or two with your favorite sauce. It doesn't get any easier, cheaper, or healthier than this.

Get a farm share. A farm share is an arrangement where you pay a set fee and on a weekly basis and receive a box of fresh vegetables, fruits, and perhaps even dairy items. Typically you don't get to choose the produce you receive—you'll get whatever is in season. Taking your children with you to pick up your weekly share and reviewing the contents of your box together is a great way to teach your kids

- where fresh produce comes from,
- the seasonality of fruits and vegetables,
- about the important work of farmers, and
- about the amazing range of fruits and vegetables and their health benefits.

Together you can figure out how to use the ingredients from this week's share in next week's meals. This is a fantastic way to encourage picky eaters to experiment with unfamiliar foods while also supporting local farmers.

Stock up on frozen vegetables. There will always be those days when you have run out of farm-fresh vegetables or discover that they have exceeded their freshness and must be tossed. Having a good supply of frozen vegetables ensures you can always serve vegetables at dinner. Many people have misconceptions about frozen vegetables, but they are fine alternatives to fresh vegetables.

Pay it forward. Cook an extra portion of dinner to take as tomorrow's lunch. When the dinner is ready, package a portion for tomorrow's lunch, and place it in the fridge. You've just saved yourself the cost of lunch tomorrow—and have one less thing to think about. With that done, serve the remaining food to the family.

Home Cooking: An Investment in Good Nutrition

There are so many good reasons to cook meals from fresh ingredients at home. Let's start with the quality of the food we serve our children and ourselves. When we cook at home, we control the freshness and overall quality of the ingredients as well as the thoroughness and cleanliness of the preparation. Just think about all the ways this practice is an improvement over eating out or ordering in.

Cooking Makes Us More Present and Less Stressed

Not only is cooking at home great for our health, but the act of cooking is also good for our mental health. Why should this be the case?

Cooking involves all the senses—sight, sound, touch, smell, and taste. As such, it roots us to the present moment. After a long day of work and/or childcare, it can be easy to get stuck thinking about something that happened during the day. Cooking helps us put those concerns aside and focus on the here and now.

Cooking with fresh ingredients forces us to slow down. The acts of measuring, washing, chopping, stirring, and searing require irreducible amounts of time. We are forced to take our time, which puts us in a less frazzled, more meditative frame of mind.

Cooking is primal. Humans have been cooking food over heat for as long as 1.9 million years ago. When we cook we take part in one of the most ancient practices of our species. It is little wonder that sharing a meal with others is associated with the pleasures of good conversation, companionship, warmth, and security.

Cooking creates a feeling of home. As the scents of dinner waft from the kitchen into the rest of the house, your children get an olfactory cue that dinnertime will be soon. This nonverbal attuning to the rhythms of daily life at home is a great comfort to children. The act of cooking shows that you are actively nurturing your family.

Cooking teaches delayed gratification. Our culture is predicated on the value of instantaneous gratification. This is ironic because most things worth having require time and effort. Cooking is a daily practice of delayed gratification and can help

Cooking at Home vs. Eating Out

COOKING AT HOME WITH WHOLE FOODS	EATING OUT OR ORDERING IN
You can ensure that the ingredients are nutritious and fresh.	The main ingredients may be fresh and nutritious, but you have no idea what additional ingredients are being used and how healthy or caloric they may be.
You can choose high-quality cuts of meat that are free of hormones and antibiotics.	Even at fine restaurants, the bottom line of the establishment is to make money. The cuts of meat you cook for your family at home are likely to be a higher quality than those in most restaurants.
You can control portion size.	Portions tend to be larger than is healthy.
You can ensure that the cooking environment is clean.	You really have no idea about the hygiene of where your food is prepared when you order in or eat out. In New York City, a recent study showed that 22 percent of restaurants had signs of mice. This was a vast improvement over the previous year, which showed the 32 percent had signs of mice. Twenty-seven percent of restaurants in New York City were found not to keep perishable food cold enough.

us see the value in looking forward to something rather than insisting it appear immediately. If it sounds like a small difference, it isn't.

The Genius of the Three-Course Dinner

Consider preparing a three-course dinner on weeknights. No, we're not suggesting that you live like you're at *Downton Abbey*, but the traditional three-course meal has much to recommend it. Essentially the three-course meal is a marvel of portion and cost control—aspects of meal planning that many Americans struggle with.

In a three-course dinner the first course is a soup or salad. This first course allows you to fill up on nutrient-rich and generally low-cost and low-calorie vegetable-based foods before you move on to the heavier and more expensive main course. The second course is the protein-based entree. Since you've had a salad or soup to start, the entree can be a smaller portion than it might otherwise be. Finally, the third course is dessert, which can be healthy (think fruit or yogurt) or small portions of something more decadent. The table on the next page spells out how the three-course meal ensures balanced, portion-controlled nutrition with benefits in terms of both calories and costs.

All in all, the three-course approach is more calorie efficient and less expensive. Because it has a beginning, middle, and end, it promotes a stronger sense of ritual than a one-course dinner does.

The Classic Three-Course Dinner

COURSE	WHAT TO SERVE	PURPOSE AND BENEFIT
First course	Soup or salad	By starting with a soup or salad, we slowly fill our stomachs with nutritious vegetables. This leaves a smaller appetite for the more caloric second course.
Second course	Protein and vegetables	The heart of the second course is a protein-rich food that fuels the body for growth and repair. Meat, fish, and tofu are all great sources of protein but are also quite expensive. We can control costs and calories when we serve smaller portions of these foods. With a first course to take the edge off hunger, a smaller second course fits the bill.
Third course	Dessert or cheese	The dinner is brought to a satisfying close with a small dessert or serving of cheese and crackers. Fruit or fruit salad is an ideal choice; other options are fine, too, as long as they're served in smaller portions.

Special Situations

- *I have a job that requires me to be accessible by phone and text, even when I am away from work. Is it okay to still remain on call by phone and text during dinner?*

If that's a non-negotiable for your job, there isn't much one can do about it. But remember: dinnertime only lasts about thirty minutes. One of the benefits of Prime-Time Parenting is that your dinner takes place at the same time every evening. So it ought to be possible to tell your colleagues that from 6:30 to 7:00 you are unavailable. It is worth trying to make that arrangement with colleagues. And it is worth asking what sort of professional culture would prevent you from doing so.

- *I have a child with Asperger's syndrome who finds it difficult to make eye contact and hug. How can I adapt the Prime-Time Parenting approach to my child's greetings?*

Because it's highly structured and therefore highly predictable, the Prime-Time Parenting approach should work well with most children on the autistic spectrum. Explain to your child the reason for the nightly greeting. Consider asking your child if you can hug her before doing so. For many children with

Asperger's, a hug can feel overwhelming. By making the structure explicit and turning it into a consistent, nightly routine, your child will grow accustomed to it and more comfortable with greetings in general.

- *I like to take some time for myself after work by taking a shower and changing my clothes before I greet my kids. What's wrong with that?*

There's nothing wrong with taking some time to yourself when you get home, but I'd greet the kids first and tell them you'll be down in however many minutes you need. When children hear a parent arrive home who does not immediately greet them, it sends a message that the parent does not want to see the children as much as the children want to see the parent. A quick hello and hug are all it takes to reverse this.

- *My child is extremely picky and will eat a very limited range of foods.*

Here's what dinner shouldn't be: a stressful negotiation about what your child will or will not eat. Children with limited palates are as old as time. It makes sense to accommodate them, within reason.

When creating your list of "fab five" meals, consult with your picky eater. Together, figure out any adaptations necessary to make each of those meals palatable for him. Explain to him the nutrients he needs to grow, and help him formulate a healthy plate of food that contains the major food groups. For some children, however, even this much accommodation will not result in a happy eater.

In extreme cases there may be an underlying issue causing their finickiness. Children may develop anxiety about eating certain foods, or they may experience anxiety in general and use food as a way of expressing it. The good news is that if anxiety is part of the issue, the predictability of Prime-Time Parenting should help soothe the anxiety. Nevertheless, when a child's choosiness becomes so extreme that each meal is a brain teaser as to how to feed him, it's time to insist that your pediatrician treat this as more than run-of-the-mill finickiness and look more closely at the potential causes of the problem.

66 When we cook we take part in one of the most ancient practices of our species. It is little wonder that sharing a meal is associated with the pleasures of good conversation, companionship, warmth, and security. 99

YOU'RE GOING TO:

- ☑ *Enjoy a relaxed and nutritious family dinner*
- ☑ *Have rich conversations with your children*
- ☑ *Encourage good table manners*
- ☑ *Give thanks for your good fortune*

Chapter Two

6:30 to 7:00 PM:
The Power of the Dinner (Half) Hour

After about twenty minutes of homework the children are hungry and ready for a break. If they're working at the dining table, tell them to clear the table of their homework things. It's time for dinner.

Family dinners are the heart of family life. Children raised in families that eat together most evenings do better at school, are more likely to maintain a healthy weight, and have higher self-esteem than those who do not. These positive outcomes last well beyond childhood.

What is it about family dinners that makes such a positive impact? In a word, it's the conversation. Although food is an essential part of the experience, it is the quality of the conversation that delivers the quality of the experience. The best family dinners are ones where people tell stories, laugh, discuss current events, have lively debates, and just enjoy each other's company. All members of the family contribute to the conversation.

The evening meal provides the perfect excuse for the family to regroup, connect, and check in with one another. Members of the family who have had a hard day can express that and receive commiseration and encouragement. Members of the family who have had a triumph get to share their happiness with the people who love them most. However the day has gone, the family dinner is the ideal venue for sharing its trials and tribulations in an atmosphere of warmth, optimism, and good humor.

Washing Hands Before Dinner

About five minutes before dinner, have your children clear the dining table of their school things and wash their hands.

It's no accident that ritual handwashing before meals is written into most ancient religions. Washing hands not only protects us from germs; it also re-awakens our senses and is a preamble to the ritual of dining.

Incredibly, only 11 percent of Americans wash their hands before meals. To encourage children—and yourself—to wash up before dinner, make it as pleasurable as possible by using fragrant, triple-milled soap that really lathers. Taking a full minute or two to thoroughly soap up, rinse, and dry hands gets the job done correctly—and is a rather luxuriant experience.

Believe it or not, there is a right and a wrong way to wash hands. The right way is:

- Use warm water, not hot.

- Use soap.

- Lather your hands as if you are making a pair of gloves with the lather. The bubbles should reach up to your wrists and completely cover the fingers.

- Take at least twenty seconds, scrubbing the backs of your hands, between your fingers, and under your nails.

- Rinse and dry your hands thoroughly on a clean towel.

- Inspect them with pride!

If your hands are wet or damp when you leave the bathroom, they are not clean. They may still have bacteria on them that can spread more easily now that they're wet. So ensuring that there are clean hand towels in the bathroom is a must.

Until your children get into the habit and enjoyment of proper handwashing, it is worth the time and effort to do it with them. Talk them through it step by step. This also gives you a chance to wash your own hands before dinner.

HOW TO WASH HANDS

Turn on warm water—
not hot!

Lather up with soap.
Go for the bubbles!

Scrub all the nooks and
crannies of hands—between
fingers and under nails.

Wash wrists with soap.

Rinse hands thoroughly.

Dry hands fully with a
clean towel.

Setting the Table

Now that their hands are clean, children can set the table. Not only is this a quick chore that children can easily learn to perform, but it will also help them mentally transition to this special family time.

It can be a lovely touch to have a few colorful (and inexpensive) tablecloths on hand to use at dinnertime. This sends a visual cue that the table, which seconds ago may have been used for homework, is now the festive site of family dinner.

Having children set the table also has the benefit of teaching them about place settings. Please see a formal place setting on page 44.

Children get two glasses: one for water and one for milk (assuming you give them milk).

The dessert cutlery goes at the top of the setting so as not to be confused with the cutlery for the rest of the meal. Soup spoons are only set if soup is on the menu.

To help your children master the art of setting the table, it is a fine idea to purchase placemats that show the place setting layout. Your child can simply use these placemats as a guide for each setting. In following this format, children learn the beginnings of table manners as well as visual organization. When they have memorized how to set the table, these instructional placemats can be taken away.

And the benefits of knowing which fork to use are not trivial. A friend told me about the time he had a big interview over lunch with an investment-banking firm. The fact that the invitation took place over lunch was telling: the prospective employer wanted to check out the applicant's manners and social

A Formal Place Setting

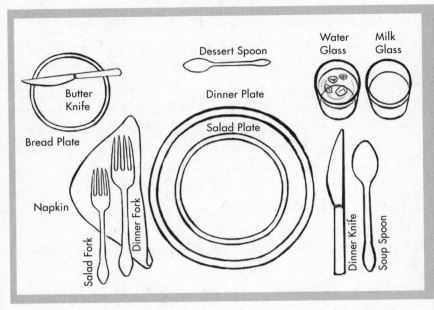

skills. My friend called his mother in a panic: he wasn't sure he remembered which knife to use when. She ended up faxing him a drawing of a place setting for him to memorize. Is this a human tragedy for our time? No, but mastering the place setting while young is one less thing your kids will have to worry about as adults when they're busy trying to impress an employer or love interest.

You'll notice the place setting above has a bread plate and butter knife. These days the practice of having bread with dinner is increasingly rare. Bread has come in for all kinds of negative scrutiny. It is worth keeping in mind that there are healthy, whole-grain breads, and when served warm, these are especially

A Less-Formal Place Setting

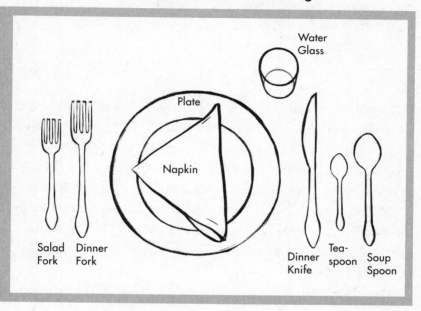

appreciated by children. If you do opt for bread or rolls, the addition of a bread plate and a butter knife adds a civilized touch to the place setting.

A less formal place setting is pictured above. It can be adapted for the adults in the family by replacing the milk glass with their drink of choice.

Lighting and Music

The family dinner ritual is your family's expression of its culture. The simple act of turning one light off in the room or using a dimmer can provide cozy dinnertime lighting. You may opt for background music that helps create a relaxed mood. The only caution is to make sure the music doesn't compete in volume with the dinnertime conversation.

Giving Thanks

The table is set. The dinner is ready. It's time to sit down.

Because dinner is a ritual, it is ideal to begin it in a ritualistic way. The ritual can be as brief as saying Grace or making a simple statement of thanks for the meal. The act of saying thanks for our good fortune—to have a family, to have nutritious food, and to have a home to enjoy both in—helps us to reset our perspective and, with it, our mood. This little ritual grounds us in the most important component of our happiness: each other.

Moreover, expressing gratitude on a daily basis is just downright good for you. People who regularly express gratitude *feel* healthier than people who don't. Because they recognize the ways in which they are fortunate, they are less prone to envy, resentment, and frustration. The daily practice of counting one's blessings discourages materialism. It makes us less likely to fall for advertisements promising us happiness through spending. Saying thanks as a family every day vibrantly adds to our sense of well-being.

Last but not least, there is never a wrong time to be grateful. When life is going well, giving thanks helps us appreciate our good fortune with humility. When life is hard, giving thanks offers us perspective. Ultimately, an attitude of gratitude fosters emotional health and resilience. We can teach our children this critical life skill every night in how we begin our evening meal.

A Connection to the Past— and to the World

Every culture and world religion has developed a ritual of saying thanks before a meal. In ancient times, when food could not be taken for granted, this daily thanksgiving had an entirely different significance from what it holds for the contemporary American family. Nevertheless, although your family may be fortunate enough to never need to worry about where the next meal is coming from, plenty of people in our country and our world suffer from food insecurity. Saying a version of Grace reminds us of this. It also encourages us to reflect on how food arrives on our plates. This awareness can only be a good thing.

If you want to find a way of giving thanks that suits your family, you might say a traditional version of Grace, create your own phrase of thanks, or adopt one of the sayings on page 48.

After the giving of thanks, dinner begins. For added formality, some families will wait for one of the parents to say, "Bon appétit, everyone!" before starting. Whether you observe this formality or not, the opening ritual sends a clear message: dinner is about more than just filling our stomachs.

Why Table Manners Matter

We've all been at formal dinners where a person has started eating before the rest of the group or taken a sip of wine before the toast has been given. Although it's nice to know the rules of etiquette to save oneself from embarrassment at formal events, this is not the true value of table manners; in fact, it's the

Thankful Phrases

For the meal we are about to eat,
   for those that made it possible,
   and for those with whom we are about to share it,
   we are thankful.

✦ ✦ ✦

Thank you for the beautiful meal we are about to enjoy,
   for our family, for our home, for our lives.
Let us consider those who are less fortunate
   and wish them strength and a better tomorrow.

✦ ✦ ✦

Thank you for this food,
   for rest and home,
   for all things good,
   for wind and rain and sun above,
   but most of all for those we love.

lowest form of table manners to make a show of noticing some-one's lack of etiquette or pointing it out to them.

That's because table manners exist not to set people apart but to bring them together. Table manners facilitate bonding. When someone burps, reaches across the table to grab the salt, or eats with their mouth open, it makes it harder to enjoy their company. In contrast, good manners are ones that don't call at-tention to themselves. If we want our children to go out into the world and find friends, we do well by them when we teach them table manners.

Between the ages of five and twelve, children should be mastering the habits listed in the table. I have made two col-umns: essential and ideal. Essential manners are the ones that help everyone have a pleasant meal. The more sophisticated, ideal manners will help your children be a delight at dinner—at home and anywhere else. I'd start with ensuring that chil-dren have the essential manners down before worrying about the ideal ones.

What Dinnertime Should Not Look Like

With all the praise heaped upon family dinners, it is important to point out that just sitting down at a table with your family, serving them food, and having some sort of verbal exchange is not enough. We have all seen family dinners on television where family members are neatly sitting around the dining table and delicious food is served while hostility seethes just below the surface. So let's look now at some common mistakes that make family dinners less enriching than they could be.

Table Manners for Children Ages 5 to 12

ESSENTIAL	IDEAL
Eat quietly. No burping or slurping.	Place your napkin on your lap at the start of the meal.
Eat neatly. Do not overload your fork or spoon.	Taste your food before adding salt or pepper.
Eat slowly.	Pass salt and pepper together, even if asked for just one of them.
Chew with your mouth closed.	Break bread into bite-sized pieces rather than biting into a roll.
Don't drink or talk with your mouth full.	Contribute to the conversation.
Don't reach for something that is closer to another person than to you—ask them to please hand it to you.	If you must leave the table, say "Excuse me."
Don't wave cutlery around while speaking (or at any other time).	Compliment the cook!
Sit up straight. No elbows on the table while eating.	When sipping soup, dip your soup spoon in and move it away from you rather than toward you before sipping it from the side of the spoon.
Do not talk over another person. Listen and wait your turn. The family dinner table has one conversation, not several.	If someone asks you a question when you have just taken a bite, gesture "one second" and take your time swallowing before replying.
No devices—including phones—at dinner. All phones should be turned off or set on silent.	Place your knife and fork together when you are finished with the meal.

Table Manners for Children Ages 5 to 12

ESSENTIAL	IDEAL
Say please and thank you.	When everyone has finished dinner, place your napkin on the table.
Use your napkin to dab your mouth clean.	
Cut your meat one piece at a time, and eat each piece before cutting the next one.	

Table Manners

1. Eat with your mouth closed.

2. No elbows on the table.

3. No grabbing the salt.

4. No burping

5. Say "please" and "thank you."

6. Don't be electronics on the table.

7. Don't fight at the table.

When Are Family Dinners Not Successful?

When the television is on. Even if the family is seated together at a table and nutritious food is served, the television pulls everyone's attention away from the conversation. And when the conversation disappears, so do most of the benefits of family dinner. Moreover, eating in front of a television makes us less conscious of how much we are eating and less aware of how full we are feeling, prompting us to eat more.

When a phone or device is on the table. Just having a phone or device on the table—even if it is off—has been shown to decrease the quality of the conversation at the meal.

When the evening meal is used as a venue for a lecture. Many parents figure "We'll deal with it at dinnertime." Sadly, this turns dinnertime into a dreaded event rather than a cherished one. Leave the lecture, if you must give one, for another time of day.

When the food police are present. Dinnertime should not feature lengthy discussions over who is eating or not eating what. If you are concerned about a child's eating habits, involve them in the planning of their meals. Some children are notoriously picky, and some children have eating disorders that require the help of a medical professional. Together, and perhaps with the help of a nutritionist or doctor, arrive at a meal plan for your child that you *both* feel good about. The dinner table should be a place of peace and pleasant conviviality, not a place of stress and scrutiny. Don't comment on how much or how little they are eating at mealtime or turn mealtime into a referendum about these issues.

When tension between parents or within a parent is palpable. Saying a version of Grace can help a parent reset their mood and remind them of what is important. Also, let children know if you've had a hard day so they won't take your mood personally.

When dinner conversation is limited to transactional talk. Conversation about tasks to be done, such as reminders of things people need to do—the upcoming quiz, the equipment needed for tomorrow's soccer game—turn dinnertime into nagging time. Think of dinner as an oasis, a time when one can forget about the nitty-gritty of everyday life and discuss topics that are larger in scope.

The benefits of family dinner have to do with a conscious choice to value togetherness, relaxation, and good conversation. At the family dinner table we are not in survival mode or efficiently multitasking our way through the meal; instead, we are living a life that we have reason to value. We are a family, not just individuals sharing the same space. We have traditions, culture, and a respite from the business of the day. As such, family dinners nourish our souls, our bodies, our minds, and our hearts. The ritual itself makes us a family.

An essential part of this ritual is the commitment to keep family dinners pleasant and positive. Parents have a responsibility to model this good mood, even when they don't feel it. The dinner table should be a place where all family members feel comfortable and relaxed. Arguing siblings should consider dinnertime a temporary ceasefire. As a parent, plan to discuss the not-so-great report card or other problems another time.

Transactional Versus Decontextualized Talk

If you've ever told your child to get ready for school, drink their milk, go to bed, or brush their teeth, then you have used transactional talk. This form of discourse is about getting the job done. We need transactional talk to function. Transactional talk is mostly about concrete things that affect the here and now. It serves a critical purpose in all our lives.

While all families use transactional talk, not all families use decontextualized talk—or if they use decontextualized talk, they don't use it much. Decontextualized talk is the language of ideas and experiences. If you've ever described something interesting that happened to you during the day, or wondered about who will be the next president, or discussed where you should celebrate an upcoming holiday, then you've used decontextualized talk.

Because decontextualized talk is more abstract, it uses a wider range of sentence structures, verb moods and tenses, and vocabulary than transactional talk. It also opens our children's minds to possibilities beyond the here and now—and beyond family life. Not surprisingly, children who grow up in homes rich in decontextualized talk do better at school. They have larger vocabularies and are more adept at abstract thinking and reasoning than children who live in homes that use very little decontextualized talk. The table further clarifies the differences between the two forms of interaction.

Transactional vs. Decontextualized Talk

	TRANSACTIONAL	**DECONTEXTUALIZED**
Examples	"Pass the salt." "Eat your vegetables." "Did you do your homework?" "Be quiet!"	"What did you learn at school today?" "A funny thing happened on the way to work today . . ." "Did you hear about . . . ?" "What is your favorite time of day and why?"
Characteristics	• Result-driven • About the here and now, things that need to happen or get done • Concrete	• Idea-driven • About experiences, thoughts, and events • Abstract

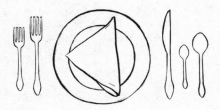

Clearly there are benefits to engaging in decontextualized talk. So how do we do it? We have simply wonderful conversations that go off on tangents, in unexpected directions, and allows us to tell stories and jokes, ask questions, express wishes and disappointments, and laugh. Great dinnertime conversations are unpredictable in a *good* way.

When parents engage in rich conversations with their children, their children's vocabularies benefit enormously. In fact, for all the benefits of reading to your children, dinnertime conversations are more impactful for their vocabulary growth. It's not just the words you use that helps children grow; it's the stories you tell, the explanations you provide, the way you answer their questions. As you talk, your children pay attention to how you articulate complex ideas and events. And as they listen, they pick up your skills. Having regular family dinners is a better predictor of high achievement scores than homework completion, playing sports, or involvement in the arts.

Kids have a lot on their minds—and lots to tell us. That doesn't mean that they always feel comfortable sharing it.

Children are sensitive to how interested we are in them and their experiences. Children pick up cues from their parents—their mood, their energy level—and adapt their conversation accordingly. If tension exists between the parents in the home, children may toe the line, or they may act up to distract and unite parents against the childlike behavior.

But it is up to parents to try to set a positive, relaxed tone at dinner when children can feel inclined to laugh and tell stories about their day.

Parents can do this by modeling their own stories. "On the way to work I saw . . . " or "I'm thinking I might find a faster way to . . . " and generate ideas. Making eye contact, listening to the person speaking, giving someone the floor is key to modeling strong conversation skills. It's also okay to say, "I had a really hard day today. Someone really hurt my feelings." As long as you are not making children feel responsible for solving your problems, there is nothing wrong with admitting when you had a bad day. The kids probably pick up on it anyway.

Eye Contact and Active Listening

When we make eye contact with someone who is speaking, we are listening not just to their words but to their facial expressions and gestures as well. One of the problems in having cell phones at dinner is that it disrupts eye contact. One second you have someone's full attention, the next they're half-listening to you while checking their phone—and soon they're not listening to you at all. It's dispiriting.

Eye contact and the respect and empathy it conveys is diminishing as a basic social habit in American culture. That's not a coincidence. As parents spend more time glued to screens, children experience less face-to-face interaction. Screen-free time allows you to model giving your full attention by giving it to your child. It will make your child feel important, seen, and heard. And it will teach them how to give that attention and respect to others.

I work with schools where teaching children to make eye contact—we call it "tracking the speaker"—is done explicitly. When the entire class knows to make and sustain eye contact with whomever is speaking, the classroom culture becomes richer, more dynamic, and more cohesive. It has to be taught by teachers because so many children arrive at school unaware that eye contact is a basic social expectation and unskilled at maintaining eye contact. This tells us that they are not receiving it at home. We can turn that around by the simple act of looking into our children's eyes when they are trying to tell us something.

Bringing the Meal to a Close

It's important that children learn that dinners have a beginning, middle, and end. As group activities, everyone stays for the whole experience. A parent can signal the end of dinner by placing her napkin to the left of her place setting and inviting the children to wash their hands. Kids will gladly do anything to delay the onset of the Homework Hustle, so they will in all likelihood scamper off in the direction of the bathroom. This gives

Storytelling

Reasonably short, amusing stories are perfect for the dinner table. And although they might not always show it, most children love hearing stories from their parents' childhood. In my experience, a surprising number of parents don't think that their childhood experiences count as "stories" or don't think their children will find them worth hearing about. Let your kids be the judge of that. The one thing most parents can be sure of is that their children will adore hearing about what the parent was like as a child. Because most parents today spent at least a part of their childhood without the Internet or cell phones, there are plenty of stories you can tell about how human beings survived without this technology.

As important as storytelling is, building on each other's stories is also critical. A part of active listening is to make connections to one's own experiences. So "That reminds me of the time when . . . " is a wonderful phrase that should be commonly used around the dinner table as one family member picks up the baton of conversation and takes the family onto another topic or story.

you and your partner time to clear the table and reset it, if necessary, with the children's schoolwork and homework kits. I recommend adjusting the lighting to your homework setting, as this truly helps children adjust their mood and behavior. Task lamps can weigh almost nothing and be moved on and off dining tables easily. They enable us to avoid lighting the room too brightly and to create a warmer, more inviting mood for study.

Parents looking for a more elaborate ritual may encourage their children to thank the cook for a great meal, help clear the dishes from the table, and say a little phrase of thanks for the dinner they have just enjoyed.

When the children return to the table—and you may need to wrangle them back from there, as bathroom mirrors and delay tactics are a lethal combination for youngsters—the scene is set for the Homework Hustle.

With children ages 5 to 13, working at a communal table with Mom or Dad makes it easier to stay on task and complete homework better and faster.

Why It's Best to Do the Washing Up Later

Most of us are tempted to take the dishes and start washing them right away. However, for the Homework Hustle to work its speedy magic, the full attention of the parents is needed at the homework center immediately after dinner. Once the children are in bed, you can do the dishes in peace, while chatting with your partner, talking to a friend on the phone, listening to music, watching TV, or in blissful quiet.

Special Situations

- *After a long day at work, I feel too worn out to be a great conversationalist at the dinner table for my wife and kids. In fact, if it were up to me, I would eat by myself! Given that most nights I am just too tired to tell stories and make interesting observations, am I doomed to fail my family at the dinner table?*

Be upfront with your children and tell them that you've been talking all day at work and now you just want to listen to their stories, thoughts, and ideas. If you show genuine interest in what they have to say, they will happily soak up your attention and keep the conversation moving largely on their own. Even if you are exhausted, you can still actively listen by maintaining eye contact, reacting to what they say, and asking follow-up questions. The key thing here is to be clear on your intent: to listen and learn from your children. To give them your full attention. Kids can always tell when an adult isn't really listening to them. If you can become a great listener for your children, you will help them reap the benefits of dinnertime conversation, even if you are a bit of a silent partner. And you'll probably be surprised to find their funny stories and observations can revive and refresh you!

- *I have no time to prepare homemade dinners for the family, much less a three-course meal. So how would I realistically prepare a three-course meal for four people on a nightly basis?*

Think vegetables, protein, and fruit. For the first course there are ready-made healthy soups at most grocery stores these days. You can stock up on canned healthy soups to use in a pinch and buy the freshly made soups when you can—or make your own on the weekend. For a salad in a rush, the packaged salads in grocery stores require little more than serving them on a plate. Your first course need be no more complicated than this. For the second course you may want to cook ahead on a Sunday or cook on the evening of the meal. Most chicken, meat, fish, and tofu dishes can be prepared in the thirty minutes you have before dinner. And for the third course a piece of fruit is just fine. Fruit is great for cleansing the palate in addition to the wonderful vitamins it delivers. Voilà! As long as you shop on the weekends to stock the kitchen, the preparation should be fast and easy.

- *I have three children, and each child has unique food allergies and preferences. How can I prepare meals for all of them?*

Work with your children (on a weekend, not on a weeknight) to develop at least five healthy meals they enjoy and run them by a nutritionist to make sure they're providing the full complement of vitamins, minerals, and protein that growing children need. Create a master grocery list with this child's favorite food and that child's favorite vegetable. It's a wonderful idea to involve children in preparing weeknight meals ahead of time on the weekend. You can even have them place their special meals in their own food storage containers. Once most of the prep is done on weekends, your family's meals may require a little more customization each night, but it ought to feel manageable.

- *Family dinner every weeknight? My kids play sports until six and need to go straight into homework. I serve them dinner at their desks, and they eat while they do homework. I just don't see this as realistic. Maybe once or twice a week?*

Although it may prove impossible to have family dinner every weeknight, we should try to have it most nights. Children need the relaxed and expansive atmosphere of family dinner to connect with their parents and siblings. The goal of family dinner, beyond the simple act of eating, is bonding, and children need that on a daily basis, not a few times a week. If activities impinge on family dinner, we should ask ourselves: What priorities are being reflected in the scheduling of a fifth-grade hockey practice until 6:30 or 7:00 p.m.?

- *If I've had a really rough day at work, I just don't feel like having dinner with my kids. I like to eat in peace. What's wrong with that? At least I don't take my bad mood out on them.*

It's important for children to see their parents cope with the reasonable challenges of life. It is perfectly fine to tell your children, "I had a really hard day today. I'm kind of in a bad mood. So I apologize if I'm a bit of a grump tonight." As long as you are not making children feel responsible for solving your problems, there is nothing wrong with admitting when you had a bad day—the kids probably notice it anyway. Having dinner together will, in all likelihood, help you feel better.

- *All this emphasis on no cell phones at dinner feels very technophobic. It's the twenty-first century. Cell phones are what we use to communicate. Isn't this all a bit old-fashioned?*

We want to integrate the best of the new with the best of the old. Good conversation is timeless and essential to our well-being. Dinnertime is an ideal venue for it. Cell phones at the table have been proven to disrupt the flow of good conversation, so we should try to leave them out of the ritual. It's that simple.

66 People who regularly express gratitude *feel* healthier than people who don't. Because they recognize the ways in which they are fortunate, they are less prone to envy, resentment, and frustration. . . . Saying thanks as a family every day vibrantly adds to our sense of well-being. 99

YOU'RE GOING TO:

- ☑ *Sit with your child as she finishes her homework*

- ☑ *Monitor your child's progress*

- ☑ *Support your child's organization*

- ☑ *Check messages sent home via backpack express*

- ☑ *Praise your child for their effort*

- ☑ *Help them pack up their school bag*

Chapter Three

7:00 to 7:30 PM:
The Homework Hustle

Before dinner, the children started their homework. Now that dinner is complete, the pressure is on to bring those assignments to completion. This is a good time for parents to sit with children and help them stay on task.

What Is the Parent's Role in Homework, Anyway?

Keeping in mind that we're discussing children ages thirteen and under, there are important roles for parents in homework completion. Parents need to:

- provide a peaceful, nicely lit homework area;

- review the assignments for the evening with their child, and let the child take the lead in organizing the order in which they will be completed;

- prompt the child to check that he has all the supplies he needs for an assignment;

- help children estimate how much each assignment will take and set timers for that estimate;

- sit with their child to ensure she stays on task;

- review the neatness and completeness of the homework, and ask for children to make corrections in these areas (but not necessarily the content);

- praise children for completing each task; and

- support children as they neatly put their homework away.

That's a lot for the parent to do. That's why throughout the Homework Hustle you'll be sitting alongside your child. You'll notice that this list does *not* include engaging with the content of the homework. If you have doubts about your son's grasp of a topic, make a mental note of it. If it continues, you might email the teacher about it. If you find a math problem confusing yourself, I'd also make a mental note of it—and wait if, over time, there is a pattern of confusing math problems before raising it with a teacher. Otherwise, I'd leave this to be sorted out between your child, the other children in the class, and your teacher. When teachers overestimate the skill

or knowledge of their students or assign problematic homework, they find out about it quickly enough without the help
of parents.

As the parent, your job is not to do the homework, comment
on the homework, or correct the homework (unless it's insisting
on neater presentation or completion); it's to support our children in seeing that it gets done thoroughly and neatly put away.

Set Up a Well-Lit Homework Center

The standard advice is that students should have a private desk,
perhaps in their bedroom, where they can work undisturbed. I
think that's great for teenagers, but for under-thirteens it is not
ideal. Children aged five to twelve benefit from working at a table or large desk with other family members close by. One reason for this is sitting by yourself as a child to do homework is
rather lonely. Another reason is that most young children don't
have the discipline to stay on task by themselves. Therefore, my
ideal homework setup for elementary and middle school children is a table large enough so you can sit with your child
during the Homework Hustle. This might be the kitchen table
or a dining room table, for example.

Lighting is important to anyone who is reading or writing.
That does not mean, however, that you have to use office-bright
ceiling lights during homework time. You can easily create a
warm, studious atmosphere with the use of a couple of inexpensive and easy-to-move desk lamps. Like anyone else, children are sensitive to environmental cues. Having a special
lighting design for the Homework Hustle can invite a quiet,
calm mood that is perfect for studying.

Timed Work Sprints

Students under thirteen benefit from using timers to complete individual homework assignments. You set the timer for the amount of time they can reasonably concentrate. Depending on the child's age and attention span, these sprints can be anywhere from ninety seconds to fifteen minutes. We call these *work sprints*. During the work sprint the child works in complete silence and cannot ask questions. After each work sprint a child can take a break of up to three minutes to clarify something about their work or to just chat.

Why no questions during work sprints? It's crucial that children learn to solve problems on their own. One of the most noticeable trends in education is the number of students who ask questions of teachers that they can easily answer themselves. It is important that children build the skill of reading and rereading directions and thinking hard about a task before they reach out for help. It is equally important that they build a self-expectation to figure things out on their own when they can.

Children who rely on adults or other classmates for help are often children who don't pay attention to the directions given for a task. I see this play out in classrooms all the time. A teacher fully explains a task. Some children are visibly not paying attention. Then, once the task begins, these children ask the teacher for directions—apparently unaware that these directions have just been given. One reason for this behavior may be low attentional control. Another may be just a bad habit of poor listening. In either case silent work sprints help enormously with building problem-solving skills and attentional control.

It is important not to confuse this approach with a lack of interest in children's questions. Asking questions is wonderful, but asking questions about things that have already been explained—or that could be easily figured out on one's own—is not. For children who really can't figure something out, they can use the break between the silent sprints to ask a parent for help. At that point they will have given a good try to understand something and the help from an adult is appropriate.

Why Is Working in Silence So Important?

In today's noisy and media-rich world it is increasingly difficult to create quiet at home, but both children and adults benefit greatly from it. People of all ages concentrate best when they are undistracted by sound. A silent environment allows the brain to direct all its resources to the task at hand.

Ironically, we are so used to noise that silence can feel unnerving and uncomfortable. The ability to tolerate and even enjoy silence—and the deep thought it enables—is a prerequisite to serious mental work. It is important to build our children's tolerance for silence so that they can benefit from its gifts. Here are just a few of them:

- Silence increases blood flow to the brain.

- Silence relaxes the brain more than easy listening or classical music does.

- Silence is an environmental cue that it is safe to disengage from the outside world. This allows us to turn our full attention to abstract thinking.

- Silence can stimulate brain growth. A 2013 study of brain structure and function found that a minimum of two hours of silence could result in the creation of new brain cells in the area of our brains linked to learning and recall.

Homework Tools
Every Child Should Have

Because parental closeness is so important to under-thirteens, the ideal homework setting is not a desk in the child's bedroom but a communal table in the home where the parent and other siblings can also work. Using task lamps for each child and observing silence during work sprints set the tone that this is homework time.

Keeping a *homework kit* in the same room as the homework center is all you need to transform a dining or kitchen table into a homework center. A homework kit is a box or case filled with all the tools a child may need to complete their assignments. This can be brought to the table at the start of the homework time.

Homework Kit

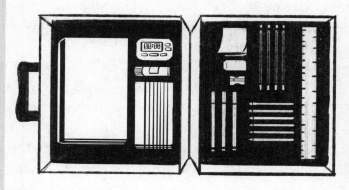

Every child needs a homework kit complete with pencils, ruler, eraser, pencil sharpener, sticky notes, magic markers, note paper, and a timer.

What should be in a homework kit:

- ☑ *children's dictionary and encyclopedia*
- ☑ *colored pencils and markers*
- ☑ *crayons*
- ☑ *erasers*
- ☑ *glitter*
- ☑ *glue*
- ☑ *pencils*
- ☑ *pens*
- ☑ *poster board (for special projects)*
- ☑ *ruler*
- ☑ *scissors*

Why Physical Proximity Helps

Children aged thirteen and under crave their parents' physical closeness. Having this half-hour working closely together is soothing and reassuring to a child. It will also discourage them from straying off-task.

It can be helpful to think of this in terms of people who work from home. It turns out that a very small percentage of people are capable of being as productive working from home as they are in an office environment. This has to do with basic human nature. When people are observing us, we tend to stay on task much better. In the same way, children who work at a communal table with a parent sitting close to them focus on homework much more easily than those sitting at a desk in their bedroom. The result is a better homework effort and, generally, faster completion.

Help Your Child Make a To-Do List

Sit down next to your child, and begin the Homework Hustle. The first thing you're going to do is take stock. Make a two-column table on a piece of paper, as pictured below, with the column headings: What has been done? What still needs to be done?

Review with your child what homework has been completed and what still needs to be done. Make two columns, and fill them out as shown above. Doing this gives your child a sense of satisfaction for what they completed before dinner and focuses them on what lies ahead. If your child did not complete much before dinner, this little chart will make that clear. It will give them a vivid visual cue of just how unwise it was to blow off the

To-Do List

What has been done?	What still needs to be done?

Done | To do

Grammar,
Math,
Vocabulary.

Science,
Reading,
Social Studies.

pre-dinner homework time. And that might just motivate them to work more effectively in the future.

Now that your child knows what needs to be done, it's time to prioritize the tasks. Let your child determine the order of the assignments, but point out that it can be smart to leave the simplest assignments for the end.

The key goal here is to help your child develop the habit of prioritization and organization. This life skill helps them feel in control and on top of things.

Next to each task have your child estimate how much time it will take. Most children (and adults) are not great at estimating how much time a task will require, so this is a worthwhile practice just for that reason. When they start completing the tasks, they'll set a timer to race against their estimate. If the assignment will take a long time, they may opt for several work sprints, with breaks in between, to complete it. Finding out how accurate their estimates are will add a motivating, interactive aspect to homework completion. Over time they'll get much better at estimating how much time an assignment will take.

As your child prepares to begin the first assignment on their list, ask them what tools they will need from their homework kit. Once they are all ready to go, set the timer and sit with them as they work.

Monitor, Motivate, Organize, and Praise

As your child completes each assignment or works to the end of a timed session, praise them for their effort. Take a look at their work. Provide feedback on its completion and tidiness. If you spot errors of the spelling, capitalization, and punctuation variety, it's perfectly fine to point these out and have your child correct them. For the most part, I would leave your input there. Your child has done his work, and the teacher will review it with the class the next day.

It is not the parent's job to do the homework for the child—or even to correct issues of comprehension. Often a well-intentioned parent will confuse their child even more by attempting to reteach a topic. This tends to happen a lot with math homework. Techniques that parents were taught are no longer being taught to today's children. Trust the teacher to correct any misunderstandings. If you're in doubt that that's happening, ask to see the corrected homework and follow up if you don't receive it.

Emphasize Persistence and Effort, Not Talent

Your child scratches his head as he tries to solve a math problem. "I don't get it!" he complains. If the parent says, "I wasn't good at math either. In fact, no one in our family is," you are promoting the idea that intelligence and ability is fixed and predetermined. If we all really believed that, there would be little point in education, which is about growth, development, and change. A comment about a child's natural ability, whether it's

"But you're so good at math" or "you just don't have the math gene" is unhelpful. It's much better to resist making comments about your child's ability in general, even when their ability is strong—*especially* when their ability is strong. Instead, focus on how they can move from one skill to the next, from one problem to the next, from strength to strength.

A much better way to support a child who is stuck on a math problem is to say, "I know math can be tricky, but I also know you can figure it out. Why don't you talk me through how you're solving the problem from the beginning?" Often that is all it takes to get a child to remember how to solve a problem—or realize that they have just forgotten the process a teacher taught them. If it's the latter, it's not your job to fill in the blanks. Typically there is a sample question that provides clues to the steps that should be taken. You can draw your child's attention to this and have them follow it as an example. If no sample is provided, ask your child to brainstorm some ways to solve the problem. If the child can't get past her impasse, tell her to move on to the next problem and ask the teacher for help the next day. You might conclude, "You can do this, but you need to know the steps. We'll look at it again tomorrow. I can hardly wait for you to show me how you figured it out."

The above approach could apply to any sort of challenge a child is having at school. We should have confidence in our children's ability to persist through difficulty and, with effort, master tough skills. It can be hard to watch our children struggle, but the struggle is a sign that they're being challenged at school, which is a *good* thing.

Have faith in your child's ability to persist through challenge, and encourage him to do so. Avoid making comments about your child's intelligence or innate gifts. It does them no favors. Instead, emphasize growth, progress, and the importance of rising to a challenge. Tell your children that real learning is going to come with hard work—and hard work is a good thing.

Independent Reading

Most children under thirteen are assigned somewhere between ten and thirty minutes of independent reading each night. Unless your child needs the full thirty minutes of Homework Hustle to complete their homework assignments, it is great to have your child use part of it to do their independent reading. Provide sticky notes so they can flag any details or events that they may want to discuss with you or their teacher later.

If you have a reluctant reader on your hands, perhaps one you suspect is not actually doing the independent reading, you might ask him to read to you or take turns reading to one another. No, this is not exactly "independent reading," but it is better than having your child not do the reading at all. Over time your child will master the skill and want to do it independently. Until then, practicing reading—which includes reading alongside a parent who is reading to you—is the way to go.

Visiting the Great Unknown:
Your Child's Book Pack

While your child is at work on his assignments, give your child's backpack a good shaking out and clean it. Backpacks sometimes resemble black holes. They are the terra incognita of childhood. They seem to have an infinite number of pockets, zippers, and nooks and crannies. Open them all, and get rid of any rubbish. Take everything out of the backpack, shake the empty backpack out over a waste paper basket, and spot clean as necessary. (It will occasionally need a machine wash, but you can leave that for a weekend.) By the time you are done with this step, your child is starting over with a fresh, empty backpack.

Things to Avoid During Homework Time

Noise. Some families are more talkative than others. Keeping the noise under control—and, yes, whispering counts—models self-control. Remember: you're only observing silence for short sprints, at most fifteen minutes at a stretch. This household discipline shows respect for homework time.

If you really can't limit the amount of environmental noise during homework time, I would invest in a good pair of earplugs for your child. They can limit the amount of noise and enable your child to focus.

Distraction. It is ideal to have short (three minutes or less) chats between assignments. Use a timer for these breaks, and when the time is up, guide your young conversationalist back to the assignment. If your youngster wants to share something important or emotional, you might say, "I can hardly wait to hear more about this. Let's get through these assignments so you can tell me all about it after homework is done." The point here is that many children, in their fervent avoidance of homework, will try to redirect your attention to something more enjoyable for them. Which is just about anything. Your consistency will help them learn to focus on what needs to be done—and not reward their impulse to avoid homework.

Multitasking. The idea that adults can focus on several things at once is one of the more counterproductive myths of our time. Many parents opt to pay bills or take out their laptops and do their own work or Internet browsing while their kids complete homework. I would advise against this. The Homework Hustle is thirty minutes of active parenting. It is hard to do two things at once well. You may get absorbed in what you are doing and fail to notice what your child is up to. If you make half an effort at supervising homework, your child may take your cue and make half an effort at doing it as well.

Complaining About the Homework, the Teacher, and/or the School

When you review your child's assignments, some aspect of it may disappoint you. Perhaps you think there's too much homework. Perhaps you feel too much of it is "busywork." Perhaps you are outraged that a question on the homework is confusing and you yourself can't answer it. You have every right to these reactions and every right to share them with your child's teacher. However, *you should not share these feelings with your child*. Here's why.

Your teacher is an authority figure in your child's life. Indeed, the younger your child is, the more your teacher represents "education" to your child. At school your child needs to follow the teacher's instructions—and if she is to do well, she needs *to want* to please the teacher and to value the teacher's opinion. When you criticize the teacher's assignments or any other part of their teaching practice, you confuse your child. It is not unlike when divorced parents badmouth the other parent to the child: it places the child in an impossible situation. The child wants to respect the teacher, and your comments interfere with his natural inclination toward respect. Now, add in any human being's natural disinclination to work when they are tired or bored, and you have a perfect scenario for a child to detach from schoolwork. Some children even learn to play the teacher off the parent. It's a dreadful, destructive, and entirely avoidable cycle. And it's too high a price to pay for your misgivings.

One of the things that our children learn at school is that a community has many members of authority—from firemen to policemen to teachers to parents. The basic civic respect for teachers should rule the day. Otherwise we are teaching that respect is optional and dependent on the parent's judgment.

Common Questions About Homework

- *The great homework debate: How much homework is too much?*

Homework is a much-debated topic among parents. At one extreme is the "no homework" movement that argues that children, especially elementary school children, are better off doing just about anything else than homework in their after-school hours. At the other end of the spectrum are schools that assign mountains of homework in the belief that this will prepare students for elite colleges. At such schools seventh and eighth graders regularly stay up until 11 p.m. finishing as much as four hours of homework.

Common sense should rule the day. Homework, in reasonable amounts, offers children independent practice in the skills and knowledge they are learning at school. It is one thing to complete a task with a teacher talking you through every step; it is another to be able to execute it on your own. That's what, at its best, homework propels our elementary and middle school children to do.

When you support your children in breaking down the organizational tasks of homework—from taking it out, to puzzling through confusing bits, to completing it, to putting it neatly away, to packing the school bag—you incrementally build your child's stamina and organizational skills. Little by little, your child will master how to analyze a task, wrestle its complexities, execute it, and ensure its neat presentation. That mastery is probably not evaluated by standardized tests—but who would doubt its value?

- *My kid gets all these worksheets for homework! That's just busywork.*

In the early elementary years children may receive homework that *looks like* busywork, such as worksheets for letter formation or simple arithmetic. It's important to recognize that what looks simple to adults may represent authentic challenge to young learners. Take those letter formation sheets. for example. By the third or fourth time a student has formed a letter on a line, are the letters improving or getting messier? That tells us a lot about the child's stamina—both mental and manual.

Young learners need a certain amount of repetition and intensive practice to acquire the writing, reading, and arithmetic skills that adults take for granted. As long as it doesn't go on for much beyond ten minutes for a first grader, twenty minutes for a second grader, and thirty minutes for a third grader, this skill-based practice paves the way for more sophisticated work. People who claim that this brisk daily practice "kills creativity" fail to recognize that the basis of all creativity is skill. And skill is acquired through practice. Moreover, when homework is assigned in reasonable, age-appropriate amounts, there is still plenty of time available for free play.

- *My child has to write an entire essay at home after a long day at school. Why wasn't this completed during class time?*

As children move into upper elementary and middle school, homework time may also be spent writing essays. This sophisticated skill requires a high level of concentration, working memory, organization, and writing proficiency. Because of that, essay writing is often best done at home, not at school. Writers need a certain amount of quiet, space, and uninterrupted time to do their work. There just isn't enough time to do it all at school. Parents can be supportive of their student writers as appreciative readers and sounding boards.

How Much Time Should Your Child Be Spending on Homework?

Grade	How much homework is appropriate?
1	10 to 20 minutes
2	20 to 30 minutes
3	30 to 40 minutes
4	40 to 50 minutes
5	50 to 60 minutes
6	60 to 70 minutes
7	70 to 80 minutes
8	80 to 90 minutes

- *My under-thirteen-year-old has hours of homework each night. It's ridiculous.*

There is one area where I agree wholeheartedly with homework critics: homework *can* be a case of too much of a good thing. The National Education Association and National PTA have provided guidelines for how long students should work on homework. Most educational experts agree that this is a reasonable guide. If your school gives a bit more than what is recommended, I would leave it alone. But if your child's school gives *twice* as much homework as is recommended or more, I would bring it to the school's attention. Communicating your concern as a caring parent is a much more successful tack than asking other parents to join you in an us-versus-them confrontation. Most schools and teachers do not intend to cause undue stress, sleep deprivation, and other negative outcomes. It is my professional experience that teachers and administrators react swiftly to parent feedback on this topic and make immediate efforts to lighten the load.

• *My child has three tests on the same day? How did that happen?*

In middle school, when teachers tend to become departmentalized, the social studies teacher may not talk to the math teacher about the homework they plan each week. As a result, students may find that their assignments, tests, and projects in several subjects all hit on the same day, resulting in homework overload and late nights for the student. Again, bringing this to the attention of teachers is always a good idea as long as it is done nonconfrontationally. Most teachers spend their workday in front of a classroom. They have extremely limited planning time to organize everything from individual lessons, to exams, to responses to student essays. This is one reason why in middle school and later on in high school you may find that your child has far too much work all due on the same day. The teachers simply did not have enough time to communicate with each other. So it's best to give teachers a (blame-free) heads-up when this happens. A reasonable teacher will modify deadlines as much as possible.

A Dedicated Pocket for the Backpack Express

During one of your three-minute breaks ask your child if there are any messages from school. Communications from you to a teacher are best handled via email because (a) you know it will actually reach the teacher and (b) it promises confidentiality. Nevertheless, there will be times when you need to send money or a signed form back to school in concrete form. It is a smart idea to use one of the small zipped areas on the exterior of your child's school bag as the designated area for home-to-school messages. This way your child can always check one spot for messages to and from the school.

Planning with Your Child

If there are messages, look at them and discuss them with your child. These normally have to do with upcoming school trips, performances, book clubs, and so on. Take out your calendar, whether it's digital or printed, and note any upcoming events, write any messages to your teacher, and place them in the designated backpack pocket.

Communicating with Your Child's School

Most teachers will provide their email addresses to parents. It's perfectly appropriate to email your teacher: "Heads-up: Not sure that Jordan understands improper fractions."

I would advise against emailing on a nightly or even weekly basis to the teacher unless there is a very significant challenge that you are working on together. I would also recommend sending emails that strike a cooperative note rather than a confrontational one.

Here's an example of a cooperative email:

Dear Mr. Sanders,

I looked over Sam's homework on improper fractions tonight. I think Sam may not have the hang of it. I didn't want to work with her on it because I may use older methods than what you're teaching in class. I did want to give you a heads-up that Sam doesn't quite have the hang of this. Any recommendations of how I can support her on this at home would be greatly appreciated.

Thanks for all you do.

Sincerely,

Sam's dad

And here's an example of a confrontational email:

Cc: Principal

Sam is totally lost in math. He has no understanding of improper fractions. I looked over the worksheet he completed tonight, and he just doesn't get it. I was a math major in college, and I don't get it either. I don't know what you're teaching in class, but it didn't work. I went on those math YouTube websites to show him how to do them, and now he is even more confused. Please call me as soon as you get this message. I am EXTREMELY concerned.

The Unresponsive Teacher

Give teachers a full forty-eight hours to respond to your emails or notes. They are almost always working with students during the day, rarely have a moment to call or email, and have a right to work-free evenings. If you don't hear back in forty-eight hours, you might call the school and leave a message with the school receptionist.

And if you *still* don't hear back, calling the assistant principal and explaining that you are trying to reach your child's teacher can be a good strategy. Explain that you have both emailed and phoned and have not heard back. A teacher who is slow to respond to a parent may not rise to an issue critical enough for a principal to deal with. An assistant principal, however, is typically much more active in supervising teachers and can handle the situation effectively.

When You Believe Your Child's Teacher Dislikes Your Child

Whatever their personal preferences, teachers have a professional obligation to treat all children fairly and equally. Most teachers meet this standard, but a few fall short. When a child comes home with stories of unfair treatment, it is wise to listen closely to them and simply say, "I'll look into it." Giving the benefit of the doubt to the teacher is important.

Schedule a meeting with your child's teacher, and ask if there is something your child is doing in class that is causing difficulties. This is a much more successful approach than accusing the teacher of treating your child unfairly. It gives the teacher an opportunity to come out and say, "Your child has great difficulty sitting during class and distracts everyone else." Once the issue is out in the open, you can work together on the problem. If the teacher denies any problem with your child, then you can share that your child has come home with the impression that she is disliked. Assure the teacher that you assumed there was a misunderstanding or a good reason for whatever the teacher did or said. At this point she will probably blurt out why she finds your child problematic. Stay calm, and ask the teacher for suggestions of what you can do with your child at home that might improve your child's behavior in school.

Leave the meeting on a positive note, saying, "I'm so glad you care so much about my child. I'm looking forward to hearing happier stories about school going forward. We'll be working on this at home. Thanks for making the time for me." If the teacher has truly bullied your child, she will be much less likely to continue doing so. You have, in the nicest possible way, let her know that you are on her side *and* on the case. If the meeting has disclosed that your child's behaviors make it hard for the teacher to work with the class, it is perfectly fine to share that with your child. Discuss how you and your child can work on any behaviors that may be problematic. Be sure to frame this discussion as cause and effect: certain behaviors cause certain challenges. Assure your child that the teacher really does like her.

When You and/or Your Child Dislikes Your Child's Teacher

Have you liked every boss you've ever had? You probably haven't. Similarly, you and your child may not like every teacher assigned to your child throughout elementary and middle school. Just as you have to do the best you can with whomever your boss is, your child has to do his best with whomever his teacher is. Emphasize your child's responsibility to do his or her best. Avoid complaining about the teacher or listening to your child complain about the teacher. Of course, if you find that your child's teachers are lackluster or problematic year after year after year, you may need to consider switching schools—or take a hard look at your own expectations.

Preventing Morning Madness: A Stress-Free Morning Starts the Night Before

As every organization guru will tell you, a great, productive, and calm day begins the night before. Once your child's homework is complete, they'll need your help—or at least your supervision as they put their homework neatly away, packing their bag for the next school day and thinking through what they might need for the following day overall—after school included. Then you can place it by the door—or wherever your "go station" is—so that there are no fires to put out the next morning. This will make it a lot easier for both of you to enjoy the rest of the evening. It may even result in a better night's sleep.

Putting Assignments Neatly Away

Your child has finished each of his assignments. Mission completed, right? Well, not exactly. Children struggle with putting papers in the correct folders and then putting the folders in their

bags without dog-earing them. That may sound persnickety, so let me describe to you two common classroom scenarios.

Scenario One. James arrives at school, goes to his classroom, opens his backpack, pulls out his folders, takes out his assignments, places them in the homework basket, puts his pencil case in his desk, takes out his lunch, and places it in his locker. He's ready for the day and he knows it!

Scenario Two. Jasmine arrives at school and goes to her classroom. She needs to be reminded to take her materials out of her backpack. She did the homework, but she panics because she can't find it. She can't remember which folder she put it in. She frantically opens each folder and rifles through it for various assignments. Then she panics even more: Did she forget to pack it? Is it sitting on her desk or table at home? Will she have to face the embarrassment of having to explain that to her teacher? Finally she finds one of her assignments. She spent a

Organized Children
Feel More Confident at School

Some children arrive at school with a neatly organized bag while others arrive with a bag that is a mess.

Guess which child had the help of a parent?
Guess which child will have a better morning?

decent effort on it, but it's all dog-eared. It doesn't look like she spent effort on it. That's because she shoved it into a folder and then shoved the folder into her bag. She's stressed, embarrassed, confused, and frustrated. And she has the rest of the day to feel the tension of not having her materials organized.

Guess which child had a parent who supervised them putting their assignments away and placing everything neatly into their backpack?

Organization plays a critical role in academic performance and is, therefore, one of the most powerful skills a child can have. And individual proclivities toward tidiness don't make the difference here—parental involvement does.

Most children under the age of thirteen don't have organizational prowess—or a burning wish to organize their backpack each evening. When a child arrives at school with a perfectly organized backpack, that's a reflection on the parent, not the child. Nevertheless, it sure has a positive effect on the child. Teachers unconsciously prefer more organized students and attribute to those students a higher intelligence level and effort than their less organized peers.

It's time, now, to work with your child on putting assignments away in the appropriate folder and then in the backpack to ensure that all that hard work gets appropriate credit. Talk your child through the process. "So we put away your math worksheet in the math folder, and then where does the folder go?" Let your child answer the question as he puts it away in the backpack. It's important both that they put the homework in the appropriate place neatly and that they remember doing so. Mornings at school can be a whirlwind, and it is easy for a distracted child to forget where he put things if parents didn't talk him through it in an explicit fashion.

Mentoring your child as she puts her assignments into her school bag takes at most five minutes. This little effort toward helping your child with organization every evening has a large impact in helping them develop organizational skills.

The Anatomy of a Backpack

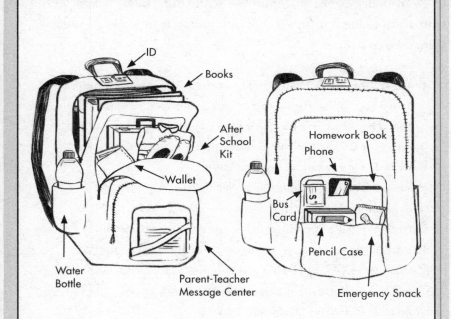

ID

Books

After School Kit

Wallet

Water Bottle

Parent-Teacher Message Center

Homework Book

Phone

Bus Card

Pencil Case

Emergency Snack

The modern backpack is an organizational wonder. Take some time with your child in planning how to best organize their things in all the nooks and crannies.

Planning the Next School Day

Now that the assignments are neatly put away, take a moment to go over the events of tomorrow with your child. As you and your child talk, chart out the day on paper. It may sound something like this:

PARENT: Tomorrow I have to go to work early, so Mom/Grandpa/ Babysitter will give you breakfast and make sure you get on the school bus. Please don't forget to give your teacher the envelope for the book club. Can you remember where it is?

CHILD: It's in the parent-teacher packet.

PARENT: Great. So tomorrow's Wednesday. What are the big-ticket items at school?

CHILD: I've got a spelling test and my science presentation.

PARENT: And you're ready for both! We've just packed up everything you need for the big presentation in science class. And you know all your spelling words. Do you remember what you do after school on Wednesdays?

CHILD: Ballet?

PARENT: Right. So let's pack up your ballet kit. *[Together pack the leotard, tights, and slippers in the special part of the backpack for after-school activities.]* Can you think of anything else you might need for ballet?

CHILD: Maybe a snack and some water.

PARENT: Good thinking. Let's pack that now. *[Together pack the nonperishable snack and water in the appointed sections of the backpack.]* So after ballet I'll pick you up and we'll go home! Looks like we're all set.

Drafting this out on paper helps model planning for your child and concretizes the various events that are coming up tomorrow. The act of writing things on paper helps both you and your child feel that you're in control of what is coming ahead. You're also helping your child visualize the challenges of the next day, which will help him deal with them.

You've both taken a big step toward a stress-free morning. And it doesn't hurt to point that out to your child. "See how we've gotten everything ready for tomorrow? That's how I know we're both going to have a great day."

Create a "Go" Station

The cherry on top of this organization is to have your child triumphantly place her backpack near her coat by the door—or wherever your "go" station is. It's official: your child is done for the night!

By the end of the Homework Hustle,

- all the homework is complete and put away,

- bookbags are packed and ready to go,

- you and your child have previewed the events of the next day, and

- your child has taken a step forward in skill development, stamina, and organization.

Special Situations

- *My child has a learning challenge such as dyslexia. She really can't do her homework without my assistance.*

There may be some assignments that a child with a learning challenge needs the help of an adult in order to complete. If this is the case, set these assignments aside for the after-dinner homework half-hour, and give your child an assignment that she can do independently during the pre-dinner homework period. That "independent exercise" might be a school assignment or something you come up with. It's important for your child's developing autonomy that she experiences the practice and pride of completing tasks independently.

- *My sixth-grader receives about two hours of homework each night. So Prime-Time Parenting does not give her enough time to complete it all.*

Prime-Time Parenting is designed for children between the ages of five and twelve. In general, one hour of focused attention to homework will be sufficient for most students in this age group. However, if your children have more homework than can be completed in one hour, you can have them start their homework earlier in the afternoon or give more time to the third quadrant of Prime-Time Parenting and put them to bed a little later. If you choose the latter, Prime-Time Parenting may last for two and a half or even three hours instead of two.

While there are some schools that give fifth- and sixth-graders more than an hour of homework, it is rare to give children this age more than two hours of homework. If your school routinely gives more than two hours of homework and it interferes with putting your child to bed at an appropriate hour, I would recommend raising the issue with your child's teacher or principal. Homework is very important, but having so much of it that it eats into a child's sleeping hours is counterproductive.

Finally, Prime-Time Parenting's emphasis on your presence and visibility while your child does homework should speed up the time it takes for your child to complete her work. Often what happens with homework is that children pretend to do it while really doing something else or drag out the process of completing it. When children really pay attention to their work, they typically do it quite quickly. Most children aged twelve and under will need a parent's presence to motivate them to stay on task.

How much homework is the right amount for the age of the child? The minimal guidelines on the table on page 85 in Chapter 3 reflect the National PTA recommendations as well as those suggested by Harris Cooper, Hugo L. Blomquist Professor of Psychology and Neuroscience in Trinity College of Arts and Sciences. I've added an upper range to reflect the habits of schools that give more homework. Keep in mind that some schools give far more homework than the guidelines here, particularly in the middle school grades.

If this is your child's situation, you will want to start homework time earlier in the afternoon if you possibly can. In the evening the Prime-Time Parenting method should help your child deal effectively with the balance of the homework.

YOU'RE GOING TO:

- ☑ *Spend thirty minutes helping your child prepare for bed*
- ☑ *Give your child a bath*
- ☑ *Read to him or her*
- ☑ *Tuck your child in*

Chapter Four

7:30 to 8:00 PM:
Bed, Bath, and Beyond

The hard work of the day is done. It's time for the restful part of the evening. With thirty minutes set aside for bath time, book time, and bedtime, we can afford to move at a gentle, unhurried pace. Bedtime rituals make it easier to wind down the day. Each ritual, from bathing to reading to tucking in, sends the body a message to prepare to sleep.

Just as dinnertime should not be reduced to the function of eating, bedtime and bath time should not be reduced to the functions of bathing and falling asleep. Instead, these rituals offer unique opportunities to connect with our children and savor the evening calm. Being fully present during this last segment of Prime-Time Parenting ensures a strong parent-child bond, a good night's sleep for our child, and the rest of the evening for you to spend as you wish.

As the best-selling book *Go the F to Sleep* indicates, putting children to bed is no easy task. Many children resist falling asleep. For the most part, this is only natural. After all, falling asleep involves surrender. To expect a child to go from wakefulness to sleep at a moment's notice is unrealistic. That's why it behooves us to spend thirty minutes guiding our children to the Land of Nod. As children progress through bathing, reading, and tucking in, the predictable practices bring them ever closer to dreamtime. That makes it easier for their bodies and their minds to fall asleep when it's time to do so.

Creating a Bedtime Routine

Predictable habits help a child fall asleep and *stay* asleep. And of all predictable habits, the most valuable for a good night's sleep is a fixed bedtime. This is called a *keystone* habit because if we can master a regular bedtime, many other positive habits are also possible. For example, if we adhere to a regular bedtime for our children, then the hours that precede bedtime take on a deliberate structure. We organize family life purposefully toward that bedtime. And when we regularly have the children in bed at the same time each night, parents benefit from nightly "me" or "us" time. This extra time for parents ensures that Mom and Dad get a good night's sleep too. Last but certainly not least, a regular bedtime makes it much, much easier for children to wake up refreshed in time for school. The best sleep schedule of all is one in which both the bedtime *and* the wake-up time is standard each and every day. It's as beneficial for adults as it is for children.

Your Child's Wake-Up Time Determines His Bedtime

Prime-Time Parenting recommends a bedtime of 8:30 p.m. for children under the age of thirteen, with a bit of wiggle room to 9 p.m. for kids at the older end of that range. This falls within the guidelines of the American Academy of Sleep Medicine's recommendations that all children under the age of thirteen should get between nine and twelve hours of sleep.

Find your child's wake-up time, and then identify their ideal bedtime.

If your child needs to wake up at . . .	Then your child should go to bed as early as . . .	And absolutely no later than . . .
6 AM	6 PM	9 PM
6:30 AM	6:30 PM	9:30 PM
7 AM	7 PM	10 PM
7:30 AM	7:30 PM	10:30 PM
8 AM	8:30 PM	11 PM

Source: American Academy of Sleep Medicine.

The Soporific Effects of a Warm Bath

Traditionally, bedtime routines for children begin with a warm, relaxing bath. As long as they don't have to wash their hair, most children happily get into the tub. It's a perfect way to begin the slow progress toward sleep.

Ancient Romans recognized the calming effects of warm water, even creating baths large enough for six thousand visitors to relax in at once. These warm-water baths healed body, mind, and soul. Roman baths were social in nature: as you relaxed, you engaged in "free-floating" conversations with a companion. Similarly, young children delight in talking with a companion while taking their bath. There is something about the warm water that encourages even the most reticent child to share. A nightly bath for your under-eleven-year-old is a precious, serene time for them to unwind, play with water, and let their thoughts drift, all while chatting with their favorite person—you.

Bath water should be comfortably warm, but not hot. Hot water stimulates the body and mind, waking a child up instead of pacifying them. About ten minutes in a warm bath should have a marked relaxing effect on your child. Whether or not she feels it, her mind and body have taken a giant step toward sleep.

Age Differences and Bath Time

While some children may be ready to bathe without a parent present at a younger age than others, a general guideline is that children under ten benefit from parental company, while children ten and older should shower or bathe in private.

Setting Up for Bath Time

In the digital age it can be easy to forget how much pleasure children derive from splashing around in a bath. It is a vivid reminder of how little children need in order to be happy: just the company of a parent, a bathtub full of warm water, and a few toys, and they are happy as a clam.

Most bathrooms have bright overhead lighting, which is not ideal for encouraging sleepiness. If your bathroom has a dimmer or lower lighting option, use it at bath time to encourage your child's natural winding down. Placing some flameless candles on the bathroom counter can also create a soothing atmosphere.

Bath toys need be no more elaborate than a plastic cup. When my son was little, a plastic filter was the source of endless bath time fascination. If you do want to shop for bath toys, this is a golden age for them. From floating puzzle maps of the United States, to complex water pipe systems and courses, to magnetic fishing rods with fish that float, to bath crayons, to the classic rubber ducky and boats, there is truly something to delight every child. A full list of great bathroom toys that encourage relaxation as well as a range of thinking and motor skills can be found in the Resources section.

The privacy of bath time and its relaxed mood and tranquility—these form a perfect break in an action-packed day for parent and child. As they tinker with their toys, children visibly relax. They chatter away to themselves and to you and will often share things unconsciously that, for whatever reason, they did not share earlier. Some of this sharing may be related to the one-on-one time of parent and child. Dinnertime was with the whole family; now they have your undivided attention.

Most children will stay in the bathtub indefinitely if we let them. About ten minutes of bath time is enough time for them to feel relaxed and languorous without overdoing it. Admittedly, as adorable as children playing in the bathtub is, it can get a bit tedious for a tired adult. Allocating ten minutes to bathing and keeping in mind how much your child enjoys it is fair to you both.

The Importance of Not Texting

Many parents text while their children are taking a bath. This reduces the parent's role to that of an inattentive lifeguard. The act of texting while a child bathes sends a mixed message, at best, to the child.

Children crave their parents' undivided attention at key points of the day. Bath time is one of them. Leave the cell phone to charge in another room while you give your children your most valuable gift: your attention.

Combining Bath Time and Book Time

If you need something to do while your child lingers in his bath, a fabulous compromise is to read your child's bedtime story while he bathes. It gives you something to do and it gives your child a chance to play while listening to you and looking up occasionally at the pictures.

A child enjoying his bath is one of life's simplest pleasures. Don't miss it by texting while your child bathes!

Grooming

When your child has finished his bath, it's time for the brushing of teeth. It's a great idea to help your child enjoy tooth brushing by letting him choose a fun toothbrush with his favorite character on it and a toothpaste that appeals to his palate. There are tons of child-friendly toothbrushes and toothpastes out there and no reason why children shouldn't use them.

By the time your child is in first grade it can be tempting to think that your child can brush her teeth without your help. However, according to the American Association of Pediatrics, most children benefit from parental help in tooth brushing until they are seven or eight. Even those children who have the mechanics of proper tooth brushing down will tend to cut corners if left to their own devices. Given the expense and the pain of dental work, an ounce of prevention here is worth a pound of cure.

Parents can help by putting the toothpaste on the toothbrush. A pea-sized amount is perfect for children between the ages of six and eight; older children will need a bit more.

Children should brush for a full two minutes. Singing a song while your child brushes or setting a timer can help ensure she brushes for the recommended time. Some children's toothbrushes even come with a music feature for this purpose. Once children are done brushing, it's wise for the parent to brush the hard-to-reach teeth in the back and check that all teeth are clean.

By the time they're six years old, most children benefit from flossing. They won't have the dexterity to floss until they're about ten, so parents of under-tens should floss their children's teeth. The top front and bottom front teeth get particular attention, as these areas are most prone to plaque and tartar build-up.

Use a face cloth to wash your child's face and ears. Give their hair a good brush or comb, and have them change into their nightclothes. Voilà! The grooming-and-bathing ritual is complete. It's time to read.

Bedtime Reading

Reading to your children as they snuggle close to you in a comfortable chair is a lovely way to end your day together.

The way we arrange a child's bedroom and the things they have in their room predispose them to certain activities. If we

All children need a bookcase all their own, filled with books representing every genre from fairy tales to graphic novels, nonfiction to novels, and reference books to classic literature.

want our child to read for pleasure, we can set up his bedroom to encourage that habit.

Ideally, you will have a quiet nook in his bedroom with a place for you to sit together and read. This is ideally a cozy arm-chair, perhaps with an ottoman. Reading to a child who sits on your lap enables us to stay physically close as we enjoy a story together. Most tweens still enjoy sitting on a parents' lap and being read to, even if they give you an eye roll or two. Someday soon they really will be too old to sit on your lap. The physical and emotional warmth do the child a power of good, especially at the very end of a day.

Every child's bedroom should have a bookcase stocked with irresistible children's books. Having a personal home "library" gives a child a sense of the riches that literature can offer. This luxury allows your child to revisit his favorite stories, consider the spines of as-yet-unread ones, and dip into unfamiliar ones that represent new territory and make them his own.

How big should a child's bedroom library be? I would suggest a minimum of fifty well-chosen books in a range of genres, from nonfiction, to fairy tales, to historical fiction, to adventure tales, legends, and fables. I'd cover a wide range of formats too, including cartoons and graphic novels, picture books, chapter books, and anthologies. Over time some books will be outgrown and given to younger siblings, cousins, or friends, and new books will replace them. Other books will remain, never to be outgrown and too precious to be given away.

Using the Neighborhood Library

Of course, a library of fifty books won't sustain a child who is reading on a nightly basis. So you'll want to make weekly or biweekly visits with your child to your local public library. In our hyper-consumer society, a visit to the local library is a wonderfully refreshing experience. Your child can select books to her heart's content, and as long as you return them by the due date, you don't have to pay a dime.

Adding a library visit to your weekend routine is a perfect way to encourage reading and exploring different topics and genres. Part of being a book lover is the joy of browsing. Let your child explore the shelves and books that intrigue her. Weekly or biweekly library visits can be especially helpful if your child's school is participating in the 100-Book Challenge or similar reading programs. Classroom libraries cannot always provide the books that are ideal for each student, and a regular library trip can fill the gap.

Moreover, libraries today have the most amazing services, from ordering books from other branches and emailing you when they arrive to providing online access to audiobooks, ebooks, and more. It would be a shame not to make full use of it.

Reading to Your Child with Flair

Bedtime reading is all about pleasure, comfort, and togetherness. And, of course, the love of a good story. But how to bring that great story alive? We need to read it with expression. And that's where some parents are more confident and enthusiastic than others.

Not all of us were read to as children. And even if our parents did read to us, they may not have read with much gusto or flair. So it's worth taking the measure of what makes bedtime reading go from serviceable to great—and that's when a parent reads *dramatically*.

Here is a quick overview of what makes for a great read-aloud performance.

Reading to children should be interactive. Pause every few pages to ask your child questions. These questions should feel natural and conversational, not academic and pressured. Good questions are always rooted in what is happening on the page, but the following ones work well for almost any book:

- What do you think will happen next?

- I wonder why [that character] did that? What do you think?

- Do you like [this character]? Why or why not?

Reading to children should be expressive. Think about the reaction you want to elicit in the child. Then emphasize key words and ideas in the text that produce that reaction. Look at your child's face to see whether he is picking up what you're throwing down.

Reading to children should be authentic. Children always know when an adult is faking. Try to be genuinely engaged in the story and read with authentic interest. Your child will be able to tell if you are bored stiff or if you are faking an emotion you don't feel while reading.

Reading to children should be suspenseful. All good narrative books, including nonfiction, carry an element of suspense. If your child doesn't want to know what is going to happen next, either the story isn't good or you need to read it in a more animated fashion.

Listening to a great dramatic read aloud is the best way to learn how to read in an engaging way. Audible is a wonderful resource for first-rate, dramatic readings of children's books. To see *and* hear a great read-aloud performance, watch Betty White, Hector Elizondo, Lily Tomlin, and others read classic children's books on Storyline Online.

Bedtime Stories: What Shall We Read?

Here's the good news: as long as it conforms to common sense about what is appropriate for children, just about anything you read to your child will benefit them.

Let your child take the lead in bedtime reading. Assuming he has done his independent reading for school, bedtime reading should include books that he chooses for fun. You may find that your child asks to be read the same book over and over again. This is actually a good sign. A child might ask for a familiar book because its familiarity reassures him or because with every reread, it delights him afresh and brings a deeper understanding. All these reasons are good reasons to reread a book. The very request shows that the child has learned that good books reward several re-readings, not just one.

After your child has heard a story or chapter from a book that she has chosen, you can offer to read a few pages from something *you've* chosen. In this way you can introduce favorite books from your own childhood or expand your child's knowledge of authors and writing styles. This is enormously valuable. Moving into a new genre or reading a new author can be challenging for a child. Many children give up on these new reading experiences far too early.

Challenging Your Young Reader

One of the lessons of reading fiction is that we often have to stick with a book before it begins to absorb us and pull us into its world. If our children give up too soon, they will miss some of the richest literary experiences on offer. Reading these books to our children gives them the support they need to plunge forward in a new literary terrain. Soon they'll be reaching for books of this kind to read on their own.

While I hesitate to suggest a programmatic approach to selecting bedtime books with your child, there are so many wonderful children's books that it might make sense to use a list to ensure that you and your child hit most of the "greatest hits" of children's literature. Or at least some of them.

Teachers do their best to share a wide range of literature with their students, but they are limited by time and the mandates of their curriculum. Fortunately, a thoughtful approach to bedtime reading can help fill the gaps.

Like a good book group, you might adapt some themes to your nighttime reading that can change every couple of months:

- fairy tales

- fables, myths, legends, and tall tales

- classic picture books

- chapter books

- biographies

- narrative nonfiction

The Primacy of Fairy Tales

If you read nothing else to your children, read them fairy tales. They are the *ne plus ultra* of children's literature—and, arguably, of adult literature too. We are never too old for these stories that have been road-tested generation after generation for centuries. More than any other genre, fairy tales are essential to an emerging love of literature and all that literature can offer us.

Think of Cinderella's plight. Or the ruthlessness of the queen in *Snow White*. Or Jack's wise credulity in *Jack and the Beanstalk*. Or the mutual rescue of Hansel and Gretel after their parents abandon them. These stories celebrate the harsh realities that modern childhood tries to conceal from children. Instead, fairy tales make clear what children have already intuited: it can be a cruel world out there, good people get hurt and some even die, and not all humans are kind and a few are diabolical. Fairy tales make these harsh truths palatable because they also tell us that with persistence, resourcefulness, and a bit of luck, even a person in a dire situation can "live happily ever after."

I used to assume that every child in the United States knew a small set of fairy tales—the ones that Disney has produced as movies such as *Snow White*, *Cinderella*, and the like. After years of visiting schools and working with hundreds of children, I now realize this is not the case. It is amazing how few children know their fairy tales. When I tell *Cinderella* to young students, it is often the first time they have heard the story. And, of course, they *love* it.

One of the most touching aspects of telling this story is looking out at a room full of eight-year-olds, all of whom are solemnly watching my face as I describe Cinderella's travails at the hands of her stepmother. The room is pin-drop quiet. When I tell how the stepmother foils Cinderella's plans to go to the ball, the children pull their own hair in frustration, punch their palm with their fists, and cry out, "She is . . . just . . . oh!" What is it about Cinderella—or any of the other great heroes and heroines of fairy tales—that makes such a claim on children's imagination?

Children, Sigmund Freud said, are "seething cauldrons of emotion." And fairy tales are worthy matches for children's intensity. When your eight-year-old comes home with the chilling realization that her best friend suddenly hates her, she may not be Snow White on the run from the cruel queen, but she suffers a betrayal as keenly as the character Snow White does.

Fast-paced, dramatic, and with life and death as the stakes, fairy tales turn on unexpected reversals and strokes of luck in the form of magic. The plot twists fire children's imaginations. They are a worthy antidote to some of the more deadening instructional practices of the contemporary classroom. In today's English language arts instruction, elementary school children are taught that all stories have a problem, a solution, and a lesson learned. Fairy tales resist such simple analysis. *Is* there a real lesson to learn from *Cinderella*? Or from *Jack and the Beanstalk*? Would we all agree on what it was? Instead of offering us platitudes, fairy tales invite us into a tangled forest of which morality is a vine, as are desire, violence, greed, courage, envy, and magic. These vines are tightly woven in fairy tales, as they are in real life. These ancient page-turners are art in the sense that Pablo Picasso described: a lie that reveals the truth. The hunger in children for fairy tales is a hunger for truth.

It is important to note that not all versions of fairy tales are equally engaging. So read them first before purchasing them, and ask your children's librarian or teacher for recommendations. I've listed my favorite fairy tale versions in the Resources section of this book. You will find that fairy tales give way to the most wonderful conversations between parent and child. You may also find—whether you were read these stories as a child or not—that these fairy tales enrich your own adult interpretation of your experiences in the world.

There are literally hundreds of fairy tales to choose from. And, of course, some are better than others. I've listed here fairy tales that, due to their sheer fascination, rich characterization, compelling plot twists and invitation to wonder, should be a part of every child's repertoire. Undoubtedly, there are many, many more wonderful choices. As Albert Einstein has said, "If you want intelligent children, read them fairy tales. If you want more intelligent children, read them *more* fairy tales."

Oral storytelling: If you are someone who can make up stories or tell fairy tales from memory, then do so. It is fun for both of you. And, after all, these stories originated as tales told orally while sitting around a fire. You can also feel free to put your own spin on the fairy tales. These stories are living things: they have changed each time a new person has told them, with details and plot points rewritten entirely in various versions. So feel free to embellish to your heart's content.

Fables

They may not have the intricacy of fairy tales, but fables pack a punch. Their wisdom and insights about human behavior may seem old hat to adults, but they are important concepts and lessons about right and wrong behavior for children.

And, as an added bonus for bedtime reading, they tend to be short. These are a great choice when your child begs for "just one more story."

Myths

Every ancient culture developed stories to explain natural phenomena such as why the sun rises in the morning and why there are stars in the sky. Passed down orally from generation to generation, myths provide a glimpse of how humans understood the world thousands of years ago in various parts of the world. Roman, Greek, and Norse myths introduce children to a pantheon of gods and goddesses who resemble the superheroes of today.

Myths expand and enrich your child's imagination while also providing them the original sources of concepts that percolate through our language and culture. Everything from an "Achilles' heel" to the source material for *Romeo and Juliet* can be found in myths.

The Must-Read Fairy Tale List

Cinderella

Little Red Riding Hood

Beauty and the Beast

Jack and the Beanstalk

Hansel and Gretel

Snow White

The Little Match Girl

The Snow Queen

The Frog Prince

Rapunzel

Rumpelstiltskin

Sleeping Beauty

The Emperor's New Clothes

The Princess and the Pea

Fables Every Child Should Know

The Lion and the Mouse

The Boy Who Cried Wolf

The Ant and the Grasshopper

The Fox and the Crow

The Milkmaid and Her Pail

The Wolf in Sheep's Clothing

The Dog in the Manger

The Goose and the Golden Eggs

The Town Mouse and the Country Mouse

The Dog and His Reflection

The Old Man and Death

The Thirsy Pigeon

Legends

What would childhood be without legends such as King Arthur and his Round Table, Atlantis, Robin Hood and his Band of Merry Men, William Tell, and the Pied Piper? These ancient stories are rooted in history, but the events they tell and even the very existence of the characters are unauthenticated. Children and adults have been riveted by legends for centuries, and their enduring claim on our imagination is reflected in the many cinematic and literary productions they continue to inspire. Legends are all about romance, heroism, chivalry, and social justice. They appeal to the big-heartedness of children.

Most legends consist of episodic stories that can stand on their own. You can read an episode from *Robin Hood* one night and then return a few weeks later for another. Over time you can cover them all.

Tall Tales

Children naturally gravitate to tall tales—stories that are full of absurd exaggerations told as if they are fact. Most children are themselves the author of tall tales and can take particular pleasure in the genre's blurred lines between fact and fiction.

Tall tales are a peculiarly American genre, so reading these fun stories with your children also exposes them to foundational characters and narratives in the American psyche.

Picture Books

Blending rich imagery with storytelling, picture books are the perfect storytelling medium for young children. Reading a

RECOMMENDED BEDTIME READING
Greco-Roman Myths

Pyramus and Thisbe

Pygmalion and Galatea

Daedalus and Icarus

Baucis and Philemon

Hercules

Atalanta and the Golden Apples

Prometheus and Pandora

Demeter and Persephone

Theseus and the Minotaur

Narcissus and Echo

Apollo and Daphne

Midas and the Golden Touch

Perseus

Orpheus and Eurydice

Norse Myths

Freya's Wonderful Necklace

The Valkyries and Valhalla

The Theft of Thor's Hammer

Idun's Apple of Youth

picture book aloud to your child is a theatrical experience. The illustration is the stage; your voice, the actors. Your child is the audience.

Just because your child is nearing his eleventh birthday does not mean he is too old for picture books. There are some fabulous ones that reward older children as much as younger

Tall Tales That Should Not Be Missed

Davy Crockett	*Paul Bunyan*
Johnny Appleseed	*Pecos Bill*
John Henry	*Calamity Jane*

children. Picture books are a visual medium, and the illustrations often carry the larger share of the storytelling than the text. Pause every few pages to ask children questions about details in the illustrations. Murmuring things like "I wonder what will happen next" or "That stepmother's not a very nice character, is she?" makes your child feel that you are as engaged as they are in the story. It also models the questioning and commenting that good readers naturally carry out as they read.

Chapter Books

Chapter books provide the opportunity to read longer stories over a series of nights or even weeks. Returning to the same story night after night is a delightful experience for parent and child. Together you get to know a character deeply over time and follow his or her development through twists and turns of the plot. As you read, swapping reactions to different events in the narrative expands your understanding of how your child thinks about the world. If something reminds you of an event in your own life, sharing that can help a child get to know you better—as well as recognize how stories help people make meaning of their own experience.

Most of us agree that some chapter books are essential to childhood. What would childhood be without the unlikely friendship that develops between Wilbur the pig and Charlotte the spider in *Charlotte's Web*? Or the sacrifice of Aslan in *The Lion, the Witch and the Wardrobe*? For a list of outstanding chapter books, see the Resources section of this book.

Biography

Biographies inspire children to think about what a life well lived might look like. They fire their ambition and introduce them to periods of time that have long since passed. Whether the subject is Cleopatra, Martin Luther King Jr., or someone still alive such as Barack Obama, reading a biography is an invitation to a wider world of events, ideas, and history.

Narrative Nonfiction Books

A much-overlooked genre of children's literature is narrative nonfiction: the wonderful telling of true stories, usually from history. These can be found in picture books as well as in longer-form chapter books for older children. Written by master storytellers, this genre is proof that the truth is stranger than fiction and every bit as compelling. In addition to piquing your child's interest in a historical event, character, or scientific invention, it provides a wonderful model to your child for academic writing. A list of recommended titles is in the Resources section.

Independent Reading

Some children, especially voracious readers, may opt to do independent reading before bed. Especially if their school requires them to read independently and they didn't get to this earlier, using the time this way is perfectly fine. I have just one caveat: even voracious readers under thirteen benefit from parents reading to them. They benefit from the shared experience, the books and genres parents may introduce that the child would never have reached for, and the discussions they can have around books.

Many schools are so happy to have a proficient, voracious reader on their hands that they don't pay much attention to the *quality* of literature the child is devouring. There is nothing wrong with your child adoring popular, commercial literature, but there is a real danger of your child not expanding her repertoire if she is left entirely to her own tastes. So I would encourage parental reading with even a proficient twelve-year-old reader at least a couple of nights a week through sixth grade. In your reading time together, you can make a conscious choice to introduce some literary texts. It may seem like an old age for a child to be read to by a parent, but it makes a valuable impact on a young person's growing imagination, tastes, and intellect.

I have seen exceptional young readers stall out in their reading development because they have gravitated exclusively to one kind of book and have never developed the persistence to read books that initially resist them.

Bedtime Chats

The reading has been done, and it's officially bedtime. A brief bedtime chat about the day that's been and the day to come helps your child ease into the pause between them.

One final saying, be it a poem, a call-and-response exchange, or prayer, concludes putting the child to bed. The body and mind love ritual and routine. Never are they so needed than before letting go of conscious thought and falling asleep.

A Proper Tucking In

We swaddle infants to help them feel safe and secure. We tuck children in for the same reason. Some children may kick the covers off as soon as we leave the room, but that is not the point. The action of tucking a child in embraces them with the covers, reminds the child that they're safe and cared for, that we see them as children, in need of our protection. Whether they kick the covers off or stay tucked in all through the night, the feeling of that parental gesture endures.

Preparing a Child's Bedroom for Sleep

Just as homework requires a suitable environment, so does sleep. It sounds obvious to say that the best sleeping environment is a dark, cool, and quiet room. In the digital age we need to work consciously to master that simple recipe.

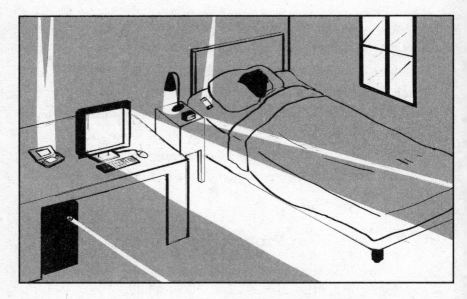

The best sleeping environment is a dark and cool one. Take stock of all the sources of light in your child's room and try to minimize any extraneous light that may interfere with sleep.

Most of our children's bedrooms have machines and gadgets that, even when in asleep mode or turned off, produce light and sound. To achieve darkness the best bet is to keep your child's bedroom screen-free. No computers or televisions, no gaming monitors—these are all much better kept in the communal rooms of the home anyway. Your child will sleep best in a room that is as dark as possible. Digital clocks or any other devices that introduce bright light into the bedroom can be edited out of the decor. Night-lights are fine because they emit a level of light that does not impede sleep.

For the same reasons, your child's small-screen devices, such as a Gameboy, tablet, or cell phone, are best stored in another room at night. When I've discussed sleep habits with children, many have admitted to playing with their devices in bed while their parents think they're fast asleep. These children were as young as nine. The problem isn't just the late-night playing; it's that the screen's blue light tricks the brain into thinking it's daytime. As a result, the hormone melatonin, which tells us it's time to sleep, is suppressed. Once the child puts the device away and tries to sleep, he is often unable to. The result is an extremely sleep-deprived child who will find it difficult to stay awake the next day at school, much less concentrate on her work.

Having a simple rule that devices are charged elsewhere overnight avoids this problem. Set up a charging station in the kitchen, living room, or wherever your "go station" is. At the same time as setting up the school bag, devices can be plugged in for charging here.

When Blackout Curtains Are Appropriate

As wonderful as a screen-free bedroom is, another source of unwanted light can come through the bedroom windows. If traffic or street lights flood in through the bedroom window, consider using blackout curtains. Contrary to their name, blackout curtains do not need to be black; they come in all colors and patterns. These thermal curtains block out light and absorb noise and air coming through the window. In the winter, blackout curtains will make your heating more energy efficient. In the summer, by blocking the UV rays, they will keep rooms cooler. For those who do not like the texture or look of thermal material, you can opt for a blackout liner and use it with a curtain of your choosing.

If your child is lucky enough to have only natural light through his window, I would resist even pulling the shade down or closing the curtains at night. As the sun rises, the natural light will give your child's body a cue to progressively wake up. This is far preferable to waking your child from a deep sleep in the dark. Moreover, having the curtains open and the shade up makes it easier for fresh air to flow into the room through open windows.

What could be better than sleeping with the windows open and benefitting from breezes that flow into the room? The more air circulating in the room, the more deeply your child will breathe while sleeping. And the more deeply your child breathes while sleeping, the more refreshing her sleep will be. Whenever possible, it's best to have the windows open at night for this reason.

In winter, even on rather chilly nights, a slightly open window is preferable to a shut one. As long as your child is well tucked in with blankets, the cool air will help him sleep deeply. In contrast, a very warm bedroom, dried out from central heating, is more likely to interfere with his sleep. While there are individual differences and preferences, the National Sleep Foundation sets the ideal sleeping temperature at 65 degrees. For some, turning the thermostat all the way down to 58 degrees at night creates an ideal sleeping environment—while also saving valuable dollars on utilities. And there is an added benefit here: when the cozy, warm bed is in contrast to the cool night air of the house, your child has an incentive to stay in bed, not get *out* of it.

For city dwellers, open windows—even slightly open windows—may introduce a remarkable increase in noise. Traffic noise, for example, can seriously detract from the quality of sleep. It is worth taking seriously: even if environmental noise does not prevent a child from sleeping, it may negatively affect the *quality* of his sleep. This in turn may produce daytime moodiness, irritability, and low concentration, among other effects. If you live in a neighborhood with a lot of traffic or environmental noise, it is worth discussing with your pediatrician ways to protect your child's sleep.

Although you can't do much about nighttime noise *outside* your apartment, you can control the amount of nighttime noise within it. I'll put it bluntly: some of us are louder than others—louder in the volume at which we speak and noisier in how we move and interact with things in our home. Many of us are unaware of just how much noise we're making and how it affects other people. For example, some parents enter their child's room at night to put away laundry. If you can do that without waking your child, that's great. But if your child is not yet asleep or wakes up when you enter the room, take it as a sign that this chore should be left for the morning.

When the kids are asleep, it's smart to consciously lower your speaking volume and try to avoid walking and talking in the hallway outside your child's bedroom. Similarly, noise from another room's TV or music can often sound curiously loud in another room. Determine a volume setting that won't reach your child's bedroom by turning on the TV or music at a volume that seems right and then standing in your child's bedroom with the door closed. If it can be heard in your child's bedroom, try turning it down. Even better, invest in headphones that allow you to watch or listen to music at a volume that works for you without any worry that it is disturbing the kids. The larger point here is to be conscious that a source of noise pollution that disrupts your child's sleep could, very possibly, be *you*.

And a last word on the topic: children are acutely aware of their parent's voices—tone as well as volume. They are intensely invested in your struggles and feelings. Don't assume your children can't hear an argument you're having with your partner just because they're in their bedroom supposedly asleep with the door closed. Make a point of having these important conversations in a room that is farthest from the child's room as possible. The same is true of animated discussions on the phone. It's best to consciously have those nighttime telephone calls as far from children's rooms as you can.

Special Situations

- *Is a nightly bath necessary for a child ten or younger?*

Unless a child has been playing in dirt or working up a sweat in team sports, she probably doesn't *need* a nightly bath. A nightly bath is chiefly beneficial for relaxation. It has the added benefit of keeping your child squeaky clean.

- *My child prefers to take a shower instead of a bath. Is there any reason why a bath would be preferable?*

There's nothing wrong with a child taking a nightly shower, but showers generally preclude conversation between parent and child.

- *The bath time routine didn't mention hair washing. Shouldn't I wash my child's hair nightly or near nightly?*

Americans tend to overdo hair washing, both on adults and on children. This can have a drying effect on a child's hair and scalp. For under-elevens, washing hair once or twice a week is recommended by the American Association of Pediatrics, and for African American children, even less-frequent washing—about once a week or ten days—is best.

Less-frequent hair washing is not only better for the hair; it is also better for bath time, as it removes from the agenda a task that most parents and children don't enjoy.

- *What about nail grooming?*

It's also a good idea to declare one weeknight "nail night," when you cut your child's fingernails and toenails. You will get improved cooperation when your child knows that Thursday is "nail night" and that it only comes around once per week.

- *When is it appropriate for children to bathe or shower on their own?*

As children near puberty, they will prefer to bathe in private. This usually happens around age eleven. You can help them create a relaxing ritual by drawing the bath for them to ensure that water is the correct temperature and mixing in some bath salts. Help them organize their bathrobe and towels—and don't ignore the possibility that under-thirteens might still enjoy playing with toys in the bath. Leave them within reach. Give them ten minutes to bathe. Not rushing them allows them some private, relaxing time to enjoy the water.

Your tweens may prefer showering and may also need to wash their hair more frequently than when they were younger. Set a timer for ten minutes, and knock on the door to let them know it's time to come out.

• *I have three children under the age of thirteen—a six-year-old, an eight-year-old, and a twelve-year-old. How am I going to give each of them ten minutes of my undivided attention at bath time?*

When you have two children or more under ten, it can make sense to bathe them all at the same time in a rowdy bathtub scene. I'm not sure how relaxing this is for anyone, but children find it enormous fun—and the soporific effects of bathing still hold.

As your children get older, group bathing, of course, becomes less appropriate. It is best to bathe your younger one first while your older one reads before bed, and then let your older one bathe while you tuck in the younger one.

YOU'RE GOING TO:

☑ *Tidy up*

☑ *Prepare for the next day*

☑ *Connect with other adults*

☑ *Relax*

Chapter Five

8:00 PM: You Time

The children are in bed. It's officially *you* time.

How much time do you have until bed? It depends on the time you need to wake up in the morning. Most adults need anywhere from seven to nine hours of sleep. Some adults can get away with just six hours of sleep, and some need as many as ten. Figure out where you are on the sleep-need spectrum. Do you require six, seven, eight, nine, or ten hours of nightly rest? Then use the table below to identify your ideal bedtime.

Once you have figured out when you need to go to bed, you know how much time you have to yourself.

Tydying Up

Cleaning may be the last thing you want to do at the end of a long day. Nevertheless, putting your home to rights can be an oddly meditative exercise.

To find your ideal bedtime, start with your wake-up time and factor in how much sleep you need.

	And you need . . .				
	6 hours of sleep,	*7 hours of sleep,*	*8 hours of sleep,*	*9 hours of sleep,*	*10 hours of sleep,*
If you need to wake at	go to bed at	go to bed at	go to bed at	go to bed at	go to bed at
5:30 AM	11:30 PM	10:30 PM	9:30 PM	8:30 PM	7:30 PM
6 AM	12 AM (midnight)	11 PM	10 PM	9 PM	8 PM
6:30 AM	12:30 AM	11:30 PM	10:30 PM	9:30 PM	8:30 PM
7 AM	1 AM	12 AM (midnight)	11 PM	10 PM	9 PM
7:30 AM	1:30 AM	12:30 AM	11:30 PM	10:30 PM	9:30 PM
8 AM	2 AM	1 AM	12 AM (midnight)	11 PM	10 PM

The first stop is the kitchen, where the dishes need to be dispatched. Now that the kids are in bed, you can do them in peace—and you get to determine whatever "peace" means to you. You might prefer washing up while on the phone, listening to music, talking to your partner, watching TV shows, or savoring the quiet.

It's remarkable how many creative people cite dishwashing or filling the dishwasher as the time when inspiration strikes.

The testimonials to the creative acts that menial household chores inspire are amazing. "I've written some of my best stuff while unloading the dishwasher because you're distracted—and yet you're not," Don Henley has observed. And Agatha Christie, the world's best-selling author of all time, said, "The best time for planning a book is while you're doing the dishes." Let dishwashing or dishwasher loading do its meditative, head-clearing, creativity-charging magic on you.

Another good reason to embrace the evening housecleaning is that it's good exercise. Housework burns about 165 calories an hour. For those of us who work desk jobs all day, the opportunity—and the necessity to move—is a good thing. Sitting for most of our workday has been linked to increased risk for diabetes, heart disease, and cancer. It also increases anxiety. In addition to taking frequent movement breaks at work, tidying up at home gives us much-needed exercise. For those of us lucky enough to have more freedom of movement during the day, end-of-day housework provides even more of a good thing.

As you clear your kitchen and the rest of the house of mess, you clear your mind. You feel more and more relaxed, as the house gets more and more orderly. For those of us who find it impossible to keep our homes tidy, there is a good chance that we simply have too many things. A cluttered home can feel overwhelming and oppressive. And by having so many things around us, we are less likely to get pleasure from the few things that we really enjoy.

How did we get here? We live in a consumer culture where we are encouraged to show love, for ourselves and others, by buying things. This puts us at risk of owning more things than we can possibly use or have room for. And then we add children to the mix, and the number of possessions in our home multiplies exponentially. We invest in storage boxes and displays when a more sensible move might be to purge our homes of things that we never use, don't need, and don't really want.

It is important to recognize when your stuff owns you rather than the other way around. A thorough clearing out of your home (best done when the kids are at school) will reveal the luxury of space unencumbered with stuff. The result will be a much neater, easier-to-maintain home. As far as toys are concerned, nobody is suggesting that you throw out toys your child adores or ones she has a special fondness for. But you probably have a good idea which ones won't be missed. And for all the unused toys you send to storage, you'll find that your child enjoys the ones that remain much more than he did before, not least because he'll be able to *find* them.

A final thought on stuff that clutters our homes: as we declutter, we begin to realize just how much money we have wasted on unnecessary items. This can prompt us to spend our money more wisely and to save more and buy less. Studies have shown what our ancestors could have told us: happiness comes from the experiences we have, not from material possessions. And many of those experiences don't have to cost a thing.

Preparing for the Day Ahead

Take some time now in the post-bedtime hush to organize yourself for the following day. Packing lunch, including beverages, to take to work can save a fortune and is almost certainly healthier than whatever is available near your office. Creating the meals for yourself and the kids and getting them all packed and ready to go is one less thing you'll need to worry about in the morning.

The digital age has not brought an end to paper mail. Each day brings a plethora of catalogs, bills, magazines, and other communications—most of them unneeded and unwanted. And laying like a needle in the haystack is the few bits of paper mail that you overlook to your peril, like a notice to serve in jury duty.

Now that the house is clean, put your feet up and rifle through the mail. Use the "touch once" approach. Toss the mail that is trash. Act on the mail that needs a response. File any mail that includes documentation you may need in the future.

Make a To-Do List

Every busy parent should have a notebook that they use for "to do" lists and reminders. This might be an app on your phone such as Evernote or a paper-based notebook of any size that works best for you. A running to-do list lets you keep track of everything in your work and family life. Now that the house is in order, take out your notebook and review the list. Pat yourself on the back as you cross out all that you accomplished today. Add any new to-dos.

Give yourself time to do a thorough brain dump by listing everything that is on your mind onto your to-do list. You may not even have an action item ready for it, but if it's on your mind, list it now. For example, you might write, "Sara's handwriting" to remind yourself that you have concerns about your daughter's writing development. You don't have to figure out just what to do about it yet, but writing it down commits it to the list of what you will act on tomorrow.

By emptying your brain of all the to-dos, you have committed your responsibilities to paper—or digital paper. Now you can set all those cares behind, especially the ones that worry you. And you can deal with it all tomorrow by starting fresh with a look at the list you've made.

Recently management bloggers have dismissed the to-do list in favor of focusing on goals and then scheduling time based on goals. There is every reason why you can and should do all three. Start with a to-do list, order which items are time sensitive or mission critical to your various goals, and then schedule your calendar accordingly. And don't forget your personal to-do items, such as getting your hair cut, going to the gym, having lunch with a friend, or visiting the doctor. Moms in particular have a strong tendency to overlook their own needs in favor of their family's or, at work, their superior's. Prioritize your needs so that you are happy, healthy, and energetic enough to engage in all facets of your life.

Preview the Next Day's Events

Look at your schedule for the next day and the rest of the days of the week. Visualize your day from waking to returning home. Problem solve any obstacles or conflicts. If something needs to be canceled, it's much better to do it the night before rather than the morning of. As parents we become much more aware of how little time we have in our workday and how finite our energies and attention span are. We become better at our jobs by applying this self-knowledge to deploy our time and energy most effectively. Consider your goals and values as you reschedule meetings and prioritize tasks. A look at the remaining days of the week helps you to maximize your time in service of your goals.

Pack Your Bag

The modern-day workbag is every bit as complex as our children's multipocket school bag. Maybe even more so. After all, different days call for different bags, which invite enormous potential for forgotten stuff. Now that you've previewed the next day's events, pack the bag you plan to take. Transfer everything you need, including your wallet, papers, laptops, tablets, keys, and any other devices. The next morning all you'll need to do is grab it and go.

Lay Out Your Clothes

Thinking through the day ahead also helps us to dress appropriately for the day to come. If we remember an important meeting with a client, which will obviously influence the clothes we wear. Lay out your clothes, including accessories and shoes, the night before. This avoids any nasty surprises in the morning when you discover a stain on the dress you were planning to wear.

Look Forward

Take a few moments to think beyond the workweek. What are the plans for the weekend? When life is overly hectic, it can all begin to feel like a blur. Now is the time to take a breath and look ahead at the next week or two. Plan the weekend for maximum fun, rest, and recharging. Is it over-packed? Are there schedule conflicts? Think through the chores such as grocery shopping and laundry. Make a plan as to when these tasks can be done most effectively—and by whom. What about that school vacation coming up? Brain-storm ideas for how you'll spend it as a family, and create a budget for the school holiday, even if there is no vacation planned. Taking the medium to long view helps remind you of all the good times that lie ahead. And that just makes you feel happier.

If it is a goal for the family to enjoy a big family vacation, one of the best things you can do is to plan it months and months in advance. This allows you to work on the trip bit by bit in the evenings, like it's a passion project. If you are going somewhere educational, the children can read books related to it, and it can be a discussion topic at family dinners. Plenty of lead time enables you to get your money's worth with the most strategi-cally chosen flights, hotel rooms, and places to visit. The time and thought you invest can allow you to avoid some of the melt-downs that can happen when children travel. You know your children, and that means you can anticipate when they will need their nap and which outing might be too much on a given day. This can have an enormously positive effect on the success of the entire experience.

Studies show that travel is one of the experiences that peo-ple enjoy the most. And part of the reason for this is that it makes us happy before the trip as we plan it and look forward to it, during the trip as we experience it, and after the trip when we share our memories with others and commit it to scrapbooks and family videos. So give yourself the gift of time to fully savor all the happiness that a family vacation can provide.

You're ready for a great day . . . and it hasn't even begun!

By following these steps you have sown the seeds for a smooth, successful morning and day. And you've done it in peace and quiet. Instead of feeling rushed and hectic the next morning, you'll feel in control and pulled together. You've also taken in the big picture. You've reminded yourself of your short-, medium-, and long-term goals, your values, and the good times ahead. With any luck, you are in a happy, contented mood.

Connecting with Others

Whether you live with a spouse or partner or are parenting solo, connecting with the adults in your life after the kids are in bed gives you much-needed support, adult conversation, and laughter. That best friend whose call you couldn't take during Prime-Time Parenting hours? You can return the call now and give her the time and attention she deserves. Your parent who lives in another state? Check in with them now that you feel relaxed and calm. This is a great time to write birthday cards or think about friends whose birthdays or anniversaries are coming up. During our active parenting years it is incredibly easy to let all this go by the wayside. Remembering our adult friends makes a big difference to them and protects friendships from the strain of inattention.

Of course, the best social interaction is direct, with both people physically present. If you are married or have a partner, share a glass of wine or cup of tea and catch up in ways that are impossible when the children are awake. Having rich conversations, including disagreements, with your significant other keeps the relationship vibrant, alive, and robust. It is much easier to have a thoughtful exchange about where to spend the next holiday or how to deal with a child's dyslexia when you are both in a relaxed frame of mind. Having it in the car on the morning commute is an invitation to a misunderstanding. Busy parents have lots to talk about with one another; setting some time at the end of each day to have those conversations can only be a good thing.

Sharing Your Troubles and Reaching for Support

The parenting years bring not only joy but also many kinds of stress—financial stress, social stress, worry over a child who has a learning challenge or a health issue, professional stress, relationship stress, and extended family stress. The list goes on and on. Even the most fortunate parents encounter difficulties and suffer real disappointments. It is important to recognize that we all need to share our feelings with people who care about us and receive support and understanding. I call these people *consiglieres*—because just like consiglieres to the mafia, these people are smart, trustworthy, and keep your confidential business to themselves.

Choose your consiglieres wisely. Every parent should have a handful of them—friends and relatives who are warmly wise and nonjudgmental. Not all friends and not all relatives will fit the bill. Before you share your misgiving about your child's persistent lisp, think carefully about which people in your life will be likely to help you—and who will, perhaps unwittingly, only make you feel worse. (In some cases, much worse!) If you don't have a few consiglieres in your deck of cards, actively seek and recruit a few. You're looking for people you admire, not necessarily parents themselves, who are great listeners and make you feel comfortable and positive whenever you are with them. It helps if they have a sense of humor.

Many mothers feel the need to present themselves as happy and successful parents. This can make it difficult to seek support when there is a problem, either at work, at home, or with one of the children. Having even just one person with whom we can unburden ourselves can make a world of difference. The great shame of keeping our problems to ourselves is that it makes it much harder to get help in resolving the issue. In most cases, whatever we're experiencing with our child has come up with other people's children. It is so much easier to get help when we can trust a few good people with our concerns. Opening up makes the problem more manageable and divests us of the burden of guilt for somehow causing the problem.

Concerns over our children's progress—whether it's their friend group, their academic work, their physical development, or something else—are always best addressed proactively. Instead of dismissing your concerns or trying to shake a sinking feeling, take the time at the end of the day to consult with trusted friends and set up those appointments with teachers or doctors to help get a handle on the situation. You'll feel better once you've taken action. Worst-case scenario: if your concerns are based on something that really does require serious attention, you're on your way to getting your child help with it.

There is nothing more personal than parenting. Each of us feels an unfathomable love for our children. The thought that we may be letting them down in any way is painful. And the guilt when something goes wrong with our children can be overwhelming, regardless of whether we have played any part in the situation. Having a genuine support system that will encourage us, strengthen us, and make us laugh in the face of difficulty is a profound necessity for every parent. If you don't have that support system in place yet, invest some time and effort in building one.

Charge Your Electronics

You may have needed your phone or computer to Skype with friends from far away or to connect via social media. Now that you've had those interactions, it's time to unplug. Set up a charging station in the kitchen or entryway to your home—someplace you are unlikely to visit in the late evening hours. Charge your devices there so they'll be ready to go in the morning.

Unplugging from our tech tools lets us disconnect from the cares and chaos of life outside our home. This makes us calmer, more content, and in control. Tomorrow, when we rise thoroughly refreshed, we can take on all the challenges, both expected and unexpected, of the new day. For now, it's time to relax.

Rest and Relaxation

There are many ways to unwind. And one of them can be to speed up a bit by moving.

Spend some time in motion. This does not need to include leaving the home. Yoga, lifting weights, running on a treadmill, or even dancing around your living room all count. Thanks to YouTube, we live in the golden age of free fitness videos. From ballet barre to swing dancing to any type of yoga, it's all available through your monitor, without charge. If the idea of getting out of your chair seems unbearable, consider setting a timer for just five minutes and staying in motion until the alarm goes off.

The benefits of movement include everything from lowered stress levels to a stronger heart, to a more robust immune function and better skin, to a more active metabolism and more energy to get through your active days.

Exercise powerfully improves mood. Movement and mood are linked *in both directions*. When people are very tired or depressed, they tend to move slowly—or not at all. Similarly, people suffering from anxiety tend to move in a way that mirrors the flight-or-fight response: they might be physically hyperactive or the exact opposite: stuck like a deer in headlights. Amazingly, the simple act of conscious moving can break us out of these low or anxious moods. The more we move, the better our brains function and the more our moods tend to stabilize. Conscious movement is any movement we do deliberately, such as dance, yoga, or tai chi.

In terms of evening exercise, take care to notice how intense activity affects you. For some of us, it burns energy and helps us relax. For others, it wakes us up and makes it harder to fall asleep. If you belong to the latter group, opt for the gentler exercises like tai chi or hatha yoga.

Get Hygge with It

Hygge (pronounced hooga) is a Danish noun, adjective, and verb with no exact translation in English, but the closest definition is a "feeling of coziness." Danes cultivate this feeling in a deliberate fashion. The spirit of hygge is a celebration of the simplest ingredients of our happiness: togetherness, good cheer, creature comforts, and a sense of belonging. And although you can—and should!—hygge alone, hygge-ing is primarily social in character. It's about enjoying the warmth of home and good company. Through the long and freezing Scandinavian winter Danes have made an art of appreciating the light that comes from candles, a roaring fire, and friendship.

When and How to Hygge

Hygge can be practiced at any time of year, but it is most associated with winter or anytime it's too cold or rainy to go outdoors. The best hygge weather is a winter storm.

Every home should have a hygge kit so that you can hygge it up when the time is right. Hygge may be about the "important things," like friendship and hominess, but it also involves a few luxuries. First things first, dim the lights and light some candles—or use flameless candles if you prefer. If you have a fireplace, light a fire. Play music that makes you happy and relaxed. Put on your best pair of slippers or cashmere socks. Make a cup of tea or hot mulled wine or whatever suits you. Then grab a blanket and a loved one and snuggle.

If you are hygge-ing alone, you may want to create a *hygge-krog*, a little nook such as an armchair with ottoman from where you can see the snow fall outside the window. Get some juicy books to lose yourself in, and enjoy the cozy splendor of reading while wrapped in blankets, sipping a hot drink, and knowing it's freezing outside.

When hygge-ing with others, board games and old-fashioned good conversation are perfect pastimes. If you are lucky enough to live nearby friends who can come by after you've put the kids to bed, spend a weeknight enjoying hygge with them. The difference between hygge and just hanging out is a conscious choice to foster and savor coziness and good cheer. This is not the time to discuss corporate downsizing, your custody arrangement, global warming, or how much you hate your coworker. Debbie Downer would not be good at hygge, so do not invite her or people like her.

Food does not have to be a part of hygge, especially if you're having it after dinner. A warm drink is enough to offer guests, perhaps with a few crackers or cookies.

Watching movies with friends can be hygge—but it is more typically about activities that enable conversation. When hygge-ing with your significant other, cuddling and reading by the fire—or in a room mostly lit by candles—is perfect. Here's what's not hygge: texting, social media, or digital devices in general.

Why does hygge make people so happy? Dr. Mark Williamson, director of Action for Happiness, observes, "The most important contributor to our psychological well-being is the strength of our relationships, and hygge definitely tends to encourage more close and intimate time with loved ones." Sometimes, when hygge-ing solo, that loved one is ourselves. And single parents *need* to hygge. A conscious act of self-nurturing improves your overall mood and mental health. People who are kind to themselves have much better mental health and life satisfaction than people who are self-critical. They also tend to be kinder to the people around them. So hygge it up.

A Good Night's Sleep

To ensure we get the most sleep and the best sleep, it's time to wind down our evening with a bedtime ritual. When kids go to bed at a reasonable hour, parents can spend much-needed time relaxing and recharging their own batteries. There are innumerable ways to relax and unwind. Here are some of the best for ensuring a good night's rest.

Meditating

The ancient practice of meditation quiets the mind and emphasizes being present in the moment. Meditation is a powerful antidote to stress. And because stress and anxiety are the enemies of sleep, people with sleep problems owe it to themselves to try meditation. By lowering your stress levels, meditation can significantly boost your melatonin levels, the hormone that induces sleep. This makes it easier and faster for you to fall asleep. It also enables richer, deeper, and more refreshing sleep.

Proven Techniques for Relaxation

Meditating

Conversation

Reading a Book

Taking a Bubble Bath

When kids go to bed at a reasonable hour, parents can spend much-needed time relaxing and recharging their own batteries. Here are some tried and true methods.

Taking a Bath

A warm bath will relax you every bit as much as it relaxes your child. Give yourself ten minutes to linger in the tub using dim light, or better yet, candlelight. Play your favorite music, and indulge in the peace and quiet. Adding Epsom salts to your bath will relax the nervous system, soothe aching limbs, draw toxins from the body, and even relieve congestion.

Playing a Video Game

While it may not strike all of us as relaxing, there is some evidence that playing video games can reduce stress. As long as you don't keep playing for hours and end up short-changing yourself on sleep, playing a video game can help you shift gears into relaxation mode.

Watching a Show

There are few pleasures quite like watching a good show at the end of a long and busy day. After all, you've done your job; you've been an active, engaged parent; you've tidied the home and prepared for tomorrow—*Now* is the time to indulge in a relaxing hour of screen time.

It's worth noting that this is a different form of TV consumption than most Americans engage in. The average American watches five hours of television a day. That much television isn't good for anyone, nor is it relaxing. In fact, studies show that watching TV when we should be talking to our children, cleaning the house, or taking care of work makes people feel bad about themselves. When people watch TV as a form of procrastination or while telling themselves that they are multitasking, it makes them anxious and diminishes their self-esteem.

But that's not you. Having Prime-Time Parented, you are in full-on relaxation mode. So enjoy your favorite show. It's not a guilty pleasure. It's just a pleasure.

Writing in a Journal

Writing in a journal helps relax the brain, preparing us for sleep. It also offers a host of other benefits that are every bit as powerful.

The way we tell our own story to ourselves plays a critical role in our resilience, good cheer, and determination. Hamlet famously said, "There is nothing either good or bad, but thinking makes it so." What we think about our lives and our identity matters more than our income level, the traumas we may have lived through, and the blessings we have received. In the privacy of a journal we get to tell our own story to ourselves. We become more aware of ourselves as the authors of our own lives. Each time we write a page, we grow in understanding our own emotions and motivations. This in turn opens the door for agency, growth, change, and coherence. Journal writing helps us cohere our past and our present while molding our future.

As Oprah would be the first to tell you, using a journal to express gratitude for our blessings forces us to recognize our good fortune. Instead of focusing on all the things we don't have and all the ways life has disappointed us, we are noticing all the good in our lives. And that, in turn, substantially improves our mood and outlook.

As a parent, you can create an extraordinary memoir of your children's childhood by writing just a little each day about them. You will treasure these written memories when your children are all grown up. As much as we believe we can never forget certain events and characteristics of our children, they are constantly changing, and it is inevitable that we will lose some memories along the way. Writing a little each night is a great preventative—and an even greater gift to ourselves in our golden years. (The kids themselves will undoubtedly want to read them too.)

For those of us who can't find our inner Anaïs Nin, there are some great five-minute journals that prompt the writer to respond to specific questions. These usually encourage us to identify events to be grateful for and reflect on the day that has passed. Try it out and see if it doesn't add to your sense of life satisfaction. A list of these journals is in the Resources section.

Listening to Music

Playing relaxing music can reduce stress by as much as 61 percent. So turn your favorite soft music on as you finish the last steps of your bedtime routine. It soothes the mind, lifts the mood, and feels luxurious, atmospheric, and serene.

Reading

According to some researchers, reading fiction is the best stress buster of all. Here's why: reading requires intense concentration.

In order to read fiction, we cannot let our mind drift. And because our mind cannot drift, it cannot introduce negative thoughts about topics that worry us. As we immerse ourselves in another world, we leave the cares of this one. As a result, we relax. Our stress levels lower. The result is a much calmer brain and body.

The health benefits of reading may include a longer life span. According to a study at Yale University, adults who read for more than three and a half hours per week were 23 percent less likely to die during the twelve-year-long study than those who did not read books.

Reading strengthens the brain, especially our memory. The habit of reading slows down the cognitive decline that happens naturally as we age and delays the advent and progress of dementia and Alzheimer's disease.

And that's just the beginning of the gifts that reading gives us. Reading literature makes us more empathic, which is a fancy way of saying it makes us nicer. Because reading a novel forces us to see through other people's eyes, we get a broader sense of human experience than our own individual life could ever provide. Consequently, when we turn to the people around us, we see them more generously. We identify patterns of human behavior with an enriched understanding of motivations and causes. We are worldlier, more humane, and kinder.

To get all these benefits, reach for a print book, not a tablet or smartphone or computer. Devices with blue light will suppress the melatonin that your body produces to tell you to fall asleep!

Time for Bed

You've tidied up, previewed the day ahead, and unburdened your brain of its various tasks and concerns. You've planned a fun weekend and have events to look forward to. You've shared your worries with trusted friends and loved ones. You've exercised, calmed your mind, and counted your blessings. You may have hygge-d. You may have watched a show or bathed while listening to music. You've read an absorbing fiction book and written a page in your journal.

The day is done. Once we've brushed our teeth and washed our face, we set the alarm clock, turn out the lights, and let sleep, which Shakespeare called "nature's soft nurse," take over.

Chapter Six

The Paradox of Structure

A routine like Prime-Time Parenting requires commitment. It reflects a recognition that amid the competing demands of modern life, we have to set apart daily time to meet our most important priorities. The choice to focus entirely on our children for two continuous hours may not sound extreme, but in practice the refusal to text, chat on the phone, or sneak in a bit of work can be surprisingly difficult. The commitment to do it is an expression of our values. It makes focusing on our children possible.

While adhering to an explicit structure may strike some as confining and exacting, the reality is it liberates and lifts us. And that brings us to the paradox of structure. A routine built around our values is paradoxically more freeing and relaxing than a looser, "anything goes" approach.

Life, let's face it, has a natural tendency toward chaos. Children get sick. Parents get sick. Caregivers get sick. After-school activities get canceled. Extreme weather events bring school closings and mass transit delays. There are early-release days sprinkled sporadically throughout the school year when your child needs to be picked up three hours earlier than normal. Childcare providers move on to new jobs. Extended family members may need attention and/or financial assistance. And that's just on the home front. At work you may be besieged with unreasonable deadlines, a demanding supervisor, and a corporate strategy that seems to change on a dime. Or you may be on the job market and surviving on a reduced income while you seek work. Amid these constantly changing seas, you are sailing your ship as best you can.

Structure helps us steady our ship. It offers us a sense of control. We can't have structure all the time—and who would want it?—but a couple of structured hours in the evening can protect our mental, emotional, and physical health.

The human body and brain crave order and predictability. When we have too many unknowns, our brains perceive the uncertainty as danger. A stress response kicks in, and our levels of the stress hormone cortisol rise. The brain interprets uncertainty as a problem that must be solved. While we are in this state it becomes difficult for us to concentrate or turn our attention to other things. We feel agitated and ill at ease.

Imagine how this plays out on a typical day coming home from the office. You've had a pleasant day at work, but just as you were about to leave you received an email about a problem with one of your projects. You don't have time to resolve the issue and you feel vaguely threatened by it. You try to shrug off the negativity as you make your way to the train. You arrive at the station just in time to watch your train leave the platform and have to wait thirty minutes for the next one. While you wait you are forced to listen to obnoxiously loud music. You ask the person playing it to turn it down, and she turns it up even louder in response. Then the train is delayed for fifteen minutes, and when it finally leaves, it is so crowded that you have to stand throughout the trip. By the time you get home, if you don't have a structure to follow, you may find yourself spent, in a lousy mood, and irritable. Nothing disastrous has happened, but your brain has had just enough unpredictability to feel overwhelmed. That's because our neocortex is designed to make predictions, and when it cannot make accurate predictions, it registers that as pain.

At this point, if you follow the well-worn routines of Prime-Time Parenting, your mood should begin to lift. Structure calms the mind, reducing stress felt throughout the body. The security of a routine helps us to regain our equanimity.

Conversely, arriving home without a plan for dinner and no set bedtime for the children would only add to our sense of overwhelm. We'd be likely to "lose it" with our spouse or our children and seek refuge in front of the TV or gaming console. The truth is that we all adhere to some form of structure, whether we know it or not. Losing ourselves in endless phone calls with friends or binge-watching Netflix for four hours *is* a structure. It's just not one that works for us over the short, medium, or long term. Unconscious structures reflect our fatigue rather than our values.

The antidote to fatigue and frustration is to build in a few meaningful routines and rituals. With a structure like

Prime-Time Parenting, we've decided ahead of time how we want to live. In our tired and spent hours, we simply adhere to the plan.

Routines and rituals are different, but in the context of Prime-Time Parenting, I tend to use them interchangeably. A routine is a set process for accomplishing something that is repeated regularly. A ritual is a routine that is invested with meaning, such as giving thanks before eating dinner as a family. Both routines and rituals are good for us. Within Prime-Time Parenting rituals and routines contribute to an overall two-hour commitment to a successful family life.

Routines Save Energy

Decision fatigue is a real phenomenon: it happens when we have more decisions than mental energy to make them. Routines prevent decision fatigue. When we know just what we're going to do and how we're going to do it, we can use our energies much more effectively. Showcasing this approach, overachievers from Barack Obama to Steve Jobs to Mark Zuckerberg have opted to wear a uniform of their own choosing every day. For President Obama it was a grey or navy suit. For Steve Jobs it was a black turtleneck and jeans. For Mark Zuckerberg it's a gray T-shirt and jeans. Different uniforms, but the same reason for wearing one. "I'm trying to pare down decisions. I don't want to make decisions about what I'm eating or wearing because I have too many other decisions to make," Obama explained. And Zuckerberg echoed the sentiment: "I really want to clear my life to make it so that I have to make as few decisions as possible about anything except how to best serve this community." When we routinize certain elements of our life, it clears a path for us to focus on what matters most. In the evening hours, when our energies are waning, routines are particularly helpful.

Rituals Help Us Live Our Values

Whatever challenges we are facing, we will face them better if we feel good about our parenting and home life. A routine like Prime-Time Parenting ensures that we invest our time in what we value. This in turn increases our life satisfaction. So rituals are a strategy for producing happiness and comfort amid the unpredictability of daily life.

Meaningful structure not only improves the *quality* of life but also can extend its length. One commonality of people who live beyond eighty-five is that they have created orderly daily lives. Long after their working lives and active parenting years have ended, these elders continue to have a daily routine that shapes their entire day and involves meaningful social interaction. Their daily routines keep them going with purpose and validation.

There is no doubt that some people are more structured by nature than others. Many of us thrive on spontaneity and freedom, but all of us can benefit from a couple of hours of structured routine each day, especially in our active parenting years. Following a structure for a few hours a night does not mean you are an automaton—quite the opposite, in fact. Most people, regardless of whether we show it or are even aware of it, are quite emotional. It is because we *are* flexible, emotional, and reactive beings that we need routine and ritual to help keep us on an even keel. Indeed, those of us on the moodier end of the spectrum will benefit most from the pacifying and soothing effect of daily rituals.

The poet W. H. Auden summed it up nicely when he said, "Decide what you want or ought to do with the day. Then always do it at exactly the same moment every day, and passion will give you no trouble."

Reclaiming Adulthood for Parents

One of the best side effects of getting your under-thirteens to bed by 8:30—or 9:00 p.m. at the latest—is that it divides the evening neatly into child-centered and parent-centered halves. The after–9 p.m. hours belong to the adults of the home—the parents. And whether you're parenting solo or with a partner, that after-hours *you* time is essential to your well-being.

When children's bedtimes are adjustable, they tend to fall later and later in the evening. As the lines blur between parents' time and children's time, neither parent nor child get what they need. The child doesn't get the structure and early bedtime that is optimal for his development. The parent doesn't get the personal time to relax and recharge after a busy day. The next morning will find them both tired instead of refreshed.

One result of later bedtimes for children is that American parents have far less couple time than their peers in other parts of the world. Each day Spanish parents spend seventy-three more one-on-one minutes with a partner than American parents do. French parents enjoy forty minutes more couple time than their American counterparts. Before you rush to attribute this finding to the longer American workday, it's important to note that American parents spend less time together *on the weekend* as well.

You don't have to be Dr. Phil to recognize that private time helps couples focus on one another. When parents spend sufficient private time together, without the children, on a daily basis, their relationships are stronger. With a healthy relationship to ground them, married parents are much better able to manage stress, both as individuals and as a couple. And all of this translates into happier, more secure children and families.

If you are parenting solo, you need private time every bit as much as married parents do. Single parents should pamper themselves each and every evening. After all, they do the work of two people in the home and are often also the major breadwinner for their children. It is a massive amount of responsibility and hard work. By celebrating your awesomeness, you let your awesomeness continue. Insisting on a couple of evening hours for yourself every night is essential. Reach out for support with childcare so that you can go out once the kids are in bed, even if it's just for an hour of two, several nights a week. Consider taking an online course once the kids are asleep to fuel your personal growth. Or practice hygge solo or with a friend or partner. By proactively insisting on your right to self-care and nurturing, you are modeling for your children how to love themselves.

The psychologist Carl Jung famously said, "Nothing has a stronger influence psychologically on their environment and especially on their children than the unlived life of the parent." When parents are unhappy, depleted, and frustrated, children unconsciously mourn the lost dreams of their parent. By insisting on *you* time, you are sparing your children that burden and demonstrating happy adulthood.

When Is Structure Over the Top?

Most of us crave a little structure, but some of us need structure a little too much. When a person is flummoxed by the smallest changes to a routine, they are considered rigid and are 39 percent less likely to communicate well with their families and 27 percent less likely to feel close to relatives.

The best sorts of structure are ones we choose to match our visions for our lives. Then structure becomes a creative tool and not an imposition. And there is no need for slavish adherence to every detail of Prime-Time Parenting. There needs to be flexibility within the frame. Some nights you may have a longer dinner than other nights or you may get home too late from work to supervise homework or eat with the children. Prime-Time Parenting does not need to be followed to the letter or followed every single weeknight, but if you follow most of its routines most of the time, you will likely reap its benefits.

Reclaiming Childhood for Children

I'll never forget the time a nine-year-old told me that his favorite TV show was *Empire*, the brilliantly entertaining, sexually explicit, and murderously violent series about a drug dealer–turned–hip-hop mogul. Is *Empire* good television? Yes, but most of us would agree that it's not for nine-year-olds. "How are you even up that late?" I asked. He shrugged and smiled.

A bit of research revealed that *Empire* isn't on all that late. It's on at 8 p.m.! To watch a show with adult language, references to prostitution, drug running, and murder, this young boy didn't even have to stay up past a reasonable nine-year-old's bedtime.

As a culture we can't seem to decide what is and is not appropriate for children. And more and more the lines between adult content and children's entertainment seem to blur. To my mind, this blurring of adult and children's spheres is worrying because it suggests a misunderstanding of the unique characteristics and needs of childhood as a developmental phase.

Children have needs that are quite simply different from those of adults. When we blur the distinctions between children and adults in one way, it can mean we blur them in others. And one thing that children need, even more than parents do, is structure.

Psychologists have long established that there are three major styles of parenting: permissive, authoritative, and authoritarian. Permissive parents are the "anything goes" types. These parents offer few rules, few demands, few limits, and lots of freedom. At the extreme, permissive parents advocate "free-range" children who get to choose whether to attend school at all. At the other extreme is the authoritarian parent: the rigid, controlling caregiver who allows virtually no freedom of choice for the child at all. And right in between, in the sweet spot, is the authoritative parent who is unambiguously in the parent role, setting routines and limitations but providing wise, age-appropriate freedom to encourage self-reliance.

The authoritative parenting style is the one associated with producing the best outcomes for children. But guess which one produces the worst outcomes? The permissive parenting style is the most damaging to child development.

Even the domineering authoritarian parent does a better job with their child than the well-intentioned, permissive one who makes few rules and confuses their parenting role for that of a friend or roommate. The children of permissive parents are at much higher risk, for example, of alcohol abuse than the children of authoritative or even authoritarian parents.

Why do children of permissive parents struggle so much in adulthood? Because their childhood lacked structure. Its free-floating atmosphere made few demands on them as children. And with fewer demands comes fewer opportunities for skill development, ranging from self-control to actual mastery of skills like setting the table, finishing an essay for school, or making one's bed. With fewer skills comes lower confidence and self-esteem as well as a lowered ability to learn how to learn.

Psychologists speculate that the worse outcomes for children of permissive parents reflect an unmet need for limits and behavioral expectations. This strongly suggests that routines are not just a luxury for children but a necessity for positive development.

Finally, there is the purely pragmatic argument for why children need structure: they have a lot to do. They need a lot of sleep; excellent nutrition; lots of parental attention and conversation; deliberate practice at academic, athletic, and artistic, skills; and free play. And that's just in the evening. How can we possibly fit it all in without a tight plan for doing so?

What Children
Want Most from Parents

In a survey of a thousand families, children were asked, "If you were granted one wish about your parents, what would it be?"

The researchers expected children to wish for more time with their parents or more parental attention. The children surprised them. The most common wish of the children was that their parents would be less stressed and less tired.

Today's parents have good reason to feel anxious. Gone are the steady jobs at companies one stayed at for decades. Gone are the healthy pensions and benefit package that came with them. Gone is a reasonable expectation that one will earn increasing amounts of money throughout one's career. And gone is the healthy adult ego that these forms of security encourage.

There is no stress quite like financial stress. Most American parents today, even successful professional parents, are feeling the pinch. In the early 1970s middle-class parents in the United States had *twice* the spending power of today's middle-class parents. And that was when most American families had only one parent earning a salary. The at-home parent managed the household, typically taking care of a wide range of chores that today's parents need to pay for.

In 2018 Americans can expect to hold ten different jobs before they're forty. For most parents, a good job and salary are the bedrock of their adult identity. When these are replaced by shifting sands, is it any wonder that today's parents are anxious? And is it any wonder that their children notice it?

There is something peculiarly toxic about financial stress for American families. The heart of the American dream is having plenty—a nice, spacious home; two cars; plenty of creature comforts; plenty of everything. For decades this has been an achievable standard of success for middle-class Americans. As it shrinks from many Americans' grasp—or arrives with unmanageable debt—the American parent's self-concept is profoundly challenged.

The parent's stress affects the entire family. It has long been established that financial stress is a leading cause of divorce and relationship strain in couples. It also strains parent-child interactions. As many as 46 percent of parents surveyed indicate they yell at their children due to stress. The less obvious signs of stress such as racing thoughts, difficulty concentrating, irritability, and avoiding social interaction are ones many parents and children experience. For all our efforts to hide our stress from our children, they pick up on it anyway. Studies have shown that parental stress weakens children's brains and depletes immune systems. Clearly, it is critical that parents find ways to lower their own stress levels so they can also lower the overall stress of their household.

Because stress is an inescapable element in life, it behooves us to find productive ways to cope with it and channel it in positive directions. Think of the ways people tend to numb themselves to the anxiety that we all feel. People turn to food, alcohol, prescription drugs, illegal drugs, binge watching, and other unhealthy activities in an attempt to self-soothe. Following an evening set of rituals that include a relaxed evening meal and good conversations is a much healthier way to resolve tension. It tells us that we are living a life that we have reason to value and that is spiritually higher than the mundane cares of the workaday world.

Following an evening ritual may be a challenge, but it is worth it. Even Kafka recognized that routine might be a clever way to extract what one wants from an uncooperative world, writing, "Time is short, my strength is limited, the office is a horror, the apartment is noisy, and if a pleasant, straightforward life is not possible, then one must try to wriggle through by subtle maneuvers."

Every step of Prime-Time Parenting is designed to support the healthy functioning of a family. It is a series of not-so-subtle maneuvers to help you enjoy family life to the hilt.

Conclusion

The Benefits of Prime-Time Parenting

Most of us start families with the expectation that they will make us happy. In theory, we could not be more correct. Studies have shown that happiness is truly based on successful relationships. A landmark Harvard study tracked more than seven hundred individuals for seventy-five years and found that the key commonality among very happy people were strong social bonds. No other element—not money, not professional success, nor social status—came close to relationships in promoting health and happiness. And of course, the relationships that contribute most to our happiness are our closest ones—our family members.

Given how critical these relationships are, it makes sense that building a warm and supportive family life should be our key priority. Investing two hours each evening in the exclusive care of your children has a transformative effect on family life. It enriches the bonds between parents and children. It enables parents to actively care for their school-age children, offering them their full attention, guidance, company, and affection. It protects family time from the unending distractions of life in the digital age.

People have different reactions to the two-hour length of Prime-Time Parenting. Most parents think it's too little time to be spending with their child. Then, when they try to devote two hours exclusively to their families, without slipping in a text here or a glance at Facebook there, they feel two hours is a very long time indeed. I agree that two hours is both short *and* long. It's long enough to accommodate the evening needs of children and families. At the same time, it's short enough to ensure that parents have time to themselves in the evening. And that's important because parents need a certain amount of time each day to enjoy aspects of their identity beyond parenthood.

Studies have shown that length of time with parents is not a great indicator of childhood happiness. If a parent is stressed, bored, or distracted while caring for a child, the child notices and in no way benefits from the parent's company. In fact, studies have shown that prolonged exposure to inattentive or anxious parents has a decidedly negative impact on children. It would be much healthier for parents to be productively employed in an activity they were interested in and actively involved in their children's care for shorter periods of the day. Keeping the evening parenting routine to an active two hours enables most parents to be both physically and emotionally present for their child. A looser and longer routine might encourage a multitasking approach, which tends to involve being physically present and mentally distracted.

So here is the good news: it doesn't take oceans of time each day to be a good parent to your child. You don't need to be with them for large portions of each day, but devoting some uninterrupted time with children, talking with them, having meals with them, reading and discussing books with them are all associated with very positive outcomes for your child's development . . . as well as for your long-term, parent-child bond.

We live in an age when American children's number-one wish is that their parents were less stressed. They wish for this more than they wish for more time with their parents. Given the challenges that American parents face, it is no surprise that many of us are anxious. Today most Americans can expect to change jobs *more than ten times* throughout their careers. Because most people don't leave jobs by choice, that means that Americans can expect to be let go or fired—an extremely stressful experience—a handful of times throughout their working lives. Furthermore, American married parents, even when both are employed, have half the earning power than married parents did in the 1970s. And in the 1970s only one parent worked in most families! For single parents the economic pressure and associated instability is even more extreme.

The resulting stress is a significant burden on parents and children. Until the underlying causes of the stress can be addressed, American parents need to find constructive ways to manage household stress. And Prime-Time Parenting can help them do just that.

A predictable evening structure provides a sense of calm and orderliness to the home. When everyone knows the order of weeknight activities, there is less household stress. By training your children's babysitter or caregiver in the Prime-Time Parenting routine, you can have the routine start at six even on evenings when you don't arrive home until later. That takes pressure off parents who sometimes work late or have social functions to attend. It also provides ongoing regular homework and mealtimes for children, regardless of who is caring for them. It buffers the inevitable changes to parent schedules and their impacts on children.

Every segment of Prime-Time Parenting—from greeting children, to setting them up for homework, to having a family dinner, to supervising the completion of homework, bath time, book time, and bed—is designed to nurture family bonds and relationships. Nobody is promising that each of these activities will be picture-perfect or that every family dinner will be heartwarming and intellectually stimulating. There will undoubtedly evenings when a child throws a tantrum and another child "forgets" his homework for the thirtieth time. But by attending to these evening activities on as close to a nightly basis as possible, parents sow the seeds of a rich and lasting family life. In fact, it's the very oscillations in child behavior from one evening to the next that reveal the routine's value. When children have regular habits and clear expectations, their challenges and moods become much more apparent—which makes it far easier for the parent to help them. In a more casual household the child's behaviors may go unnoticed and undealt with.

Predictable family time each evening has benefits beyond the present. They establish a pattern of convivial behavior that will make it more likely your children will go on to build robust families of their own. More than anything else, these strong familial bonds are likely to predict their health, happiness, and life satisfaction throughout their lives. As Robert Waldinger, the director of the Harvard Study of Adult Development, commented about the study of more than 724 men for seventy-five years, "The clearest message we get from this 75 year study is this: good relationships keep us happier and healthier. Period."

Prime-Time Parenting also emphasizes the need for parents to set aside time for self-care. This is possible because the children have gone to bed at a reasonable hour. Actively caring for one another and for one's self promotes mental health because it helps us to repair the damages of the day. If we've had a major disappointment, we can reach out for support from other adults to process it and move on. Imagine the alternative: a parent who does not have the time or privacy to converse with other adults is more likely to turn her own child into a confidante, which is a distortion of the parent-child relationship. It is critical that parents have time and opportunity to get the support they need from other adults. When they don't, their children sense their pain and isolation, and it burdens them.

Even though Prime-Time Parenting is a two-hour routine for families, it probably should be described as a four-hour evening routine. After the two hours with the children, the time for the parents is every bit as important—the essential opportunity to ensure that parents are as well looked after as their children.

Physical Health

Ensuring that your child eats a nutritious meal and gets a good night's sleep makes it more likely that you, the parent, will do the same. Both nutrition and adequate sleep support mental health. In times of great stress our eating and sleeping habits can take a hit. We might overeat and/or eat unhealthy foods. Sleep, which can do us so much good, can elude us. The formal family dinner advocated in Prime-Time Parenting makes it less likely that a parent will stress eat or change one's patterns of consumption. The bedtime routines set out in Prime-Time Parenting enables us to cope better with the stressors we face. Moreover, the balanced approach to caring for children and caring for ourselves, including exercising and seeking adult connection, are all very much in keeping with best practices for maintaining strong mental health.

Studies of people who live into advanced old age (over one hundred) show that they tend to live orderly lives with a set routine that shapes their days. Experts say that it's no accident that the structure of daily routines promotes longevity. First, routines reduce stress, which improves the immune function. Second, when the body enacts the same set of healthy rituals, more or less, each day, the body has less mileage than its years might suggest. Needless to say, the daily rituals must be healthy ones: ones that involve a certain amount of social interaction, physical exercise, and mental stimulation.

The role of pleasure to maintaining physical health is often overlooked. Physical experiences such as taking a long bubble bath, getting a massage, and laughing uproariously all release positive sensations that make us healthier, more alive, and vibrant. We can't leave these experiences to chance; we have to actively cultivate them—just as the Danish cultivate hygge. By having a good two hours to ourselves after the children are asleep, we can do just that.

Emotional Health

Happiness is not the removal of conflict, challenge, or stress. A life well lived has plenty of conflict, challenge, and stress. Happiness does not mean that all your personal needs are met either—some of the happiest people in the world have very little, indeed.

Rather, happiness is the result of gratitude and appreciation for what we do have, whatever that is. It's the way we *think* about our lives that make us happy. And so it is possible to be enormously wealthy and utterly miserable at the same time. It is also possible to have very little and be very happy. Clearly we would all benefit from practicing gratitude on a daily basis. Prime-Time Parenting supports this outlook through advocating rituals of grace before dinner and counting our blessings before bed. These nightly practices work their magic on children's happiness as well as on our own.

We live in a culture that constantly tries to convince us we need to spend money to experience happiness. As a result, our feelings of desire, envy, and even greed are continually animated to prompt us to transfer money out of our bank accounts and into someone else's. This does not lead us to happiness, and over the medium and long term it does not make us feel in control either. Cultivating gratitude and appreciation does both.

As the landmark seventy-five-year Harvard study of adult development proved, our relationships make us happy. They are the area worth investing our time, energy, and creativity if we are going to live happy lives.

If you were born into a wonderfully supportive family, whether it was rich, poor, or average, you were born with the greatest gift imaginable. If you were less fortunate and have a family of origin mired in conflict or even nonexistent, then you may have to work hard to build a supportive community that grounds and uplifts you. The good news here is that you can consciously and carefully recruit people whose qualities you admire. A circle of ten reliable friends, colleagues, and neighbors creates a community that envelops you with goodwill, care, and support. Give at least as much as you receive from these relationships. They support your emotional health as well as your children's.

The arrival of children, though a source of great joy, necessarily changes the relationship between its parents. Whereas before the couple had the freedom to devote lots of time to one another and the financial resources to go out to dinner regularly and take wonderful, romantic vacations, now the couple focuses most of its resources on their children. They spend less time relating to one another as lovers. In general, they have sex less frequently and report a steep decline in relationship satisfaction. Moreover, the financial stress of their children combined with the organizational hurdles of combining work and childcare and their inevitable fatigue can take its toll on a parents' health and mood.

It stands to reason that the relationship between the parents is the most important relationship within the family. After all, it is well established that being raised in a happy household with two parents who love one another benefits children more than any other family structure. The economies of scale that come with a two-parent household make all of the parents' resources—time, money, and energy—go much further than if they were parenting independently. All of this is to say that parents need to cultivate their relationship while also looking after their children—their families and their own individual happiness depend on it.

Prime-Time Parenting can help with three of the challenges parents face in nurturing their relationship with one another:

- sharing parenting duties more equally

- cultivating family rituals that strengthen their bond

- protecting their one-on-one time

Parenting in the Evenings Together

An enormous source of resentment within relationships is the sense that one parent is doing most of the household and child-rearing work. This can start out quite innocently with the basic division of labor: one parent spends more time at work, playing the role of provider, and the other parent spends more time with the children, playing the role of the caregiver. There is nothing wrong with this division of labor as long as there is a part of the day when both parents *parent together*. The last thing most at-home parents want to see at the end of a long day of caring for children is their partner arriving home and yearning to relax in a way that leaves the caregiver with the second shift to do solo.

Parenting requires discipline. Having both parents agree on a structure like Prime-Time Parenting allows them to parent for two hours a day together. They set aside their fatigue and devote themselves for two hours to active parenting, with the awareness that they will get their well-earned relaxation time at the end of it. When both parents cook together, eat together, and supervise homework, bath, book, and bedtime together, it absolutely transforms the family culture. The last hours of the parenting day become precious family time, and parents become true partners and companions. One of the hardest aspects of caring for children is the absence of adult company and conversation. The addition of the other parent to the final phases of the child's day gives a real boost to the parent who does the larger share of the caregiving. It also helps the "provider" parent to fully appreciate just how much their caregiving partner does.

While it is ideal that parents share fifty-fifty of the childcare responsibilities, in practice there is almost always a parent who takes the role of primary caregiver, even if that parent also works full time. The parent who does relatively less of the childcare and household work may envy their child for receiving so much of the other parent's love and affection. Or they may just feel a bit neglected and less important to their partner than the children. The best antidote to this feeling? Do some of the childcare and household chores on a nightly basis together.

Sharing time with children as they do their work or read before bed enables you both to notice how adorable your children are. Instead of having to describe something your child said or did to the absent parent, you can both witness it. Exchanging glances after your child has expressed a wonderful observation or done something funny adds magic to your parenting relationship. You are in this together—and it feels that way.

Creating Family Rituals

Your family has rituals whether you know it or not. It's just that its current rituals may not reflect your true values and beliefs. If your children watch too much television or spend excessive hours playing video games before you finally put them to bed, that is a ritual. It's probably not a ritual you feel very good about, which also makes you feel not very good about yourself.

When we actively devote two hours each evening to our families, we consciously create rituals, such as family dinner, that make us feel good about the lives we're leading. That adds an enormous boost to our happiness. It connects the way we live to our most deeply held values. It rightly makes us feel that we are successful as parents. And it brings daily happiness to the otherwise mundane functions of eating and getting ready for bed.

By following the routines within Prime-Time Parenting, you and your partner can feel successful as parents regardless of what else might be going on in the world or in your professional lives. You are actively building a family that knows what is most important and lives accordingly. That's one of the greatest life satisfactions that anyone can have. And it doesn't cost a dime to make it happen.

Protecting One-on-One Time

The discipline of doing the impossible—putting the children to bed at a reasonable hour—gives you two the rest of the evening to be together as a couple. Absolute clarity on bedtime and a lack of indulgence to children who want repeated curtain calls protects this valuable time. Now you can enjoy each other's company in peace and privacy.

The biggest predictor of overall life satisfaction is your happiness with your life partner. So nurture your time together by both parenting together in the evenings and following a structure that protects your own private time. There are few better ways to ensure the happiness of your family than by setting aside an hour or two each night for one another.

Resources to Support Prime-Time Parenting

Chapter 1:
6:00 to 6:30 PM: Prime-Time Parenting Begins

For Organizing Homework and Schedules

Any notebook will do, but the following resources can add an element of fun to organizing and planning.

TO-DO LISTS

Let's Do This! Notepad, at riflepaperco.com
Desktop Tear-Off Notepad, at riflepaperco.com

WEEKLY PLANNERS

Twone Animal Weekly Planner, from Organizers for Kids
Wild at Heart Desk Pad Weekly Planner, available at
   Anthropologie

TIMERS

Children need to "see" time pass. These timers all do an excellent job of helping children view the passage of time.

Uglydoll School Planner Spiral-Bound, by David Horvath
Teacher Created Resources Small Sand Timers Combo Pack
Veoley 10-Minute Sand Timer
Rectangular Liquid Motion Timer Toy for Sensory Play
Neliblu: Liquid Water Wheel Timer Toy

For Creating a Homework Center

It's ideal to use a dining table or kitchen table for homework because parents and children can sit around it together. To transform the table into a homework center, you need a few portable work lamps and a homework kit that contains all the supplies a child is likely to need. The list below contains all you should need to create a portable homework kit.

PORTABLE WORK LAMPS

> Ikea Snoig Work lamp
> Jangsjo LED Work Lamp

CONTAINERS TO STORE HOMEWORK SUPPLIES

> Ikea KUGGIS box with lid
> Ikea KUGGIS insert with eight compartments

DESK PAD

> Ikea Projs Desk pad

HOMEWORK SUPPLY PACK

One-stop shopping for all the supplies your child will need to complete homework:

> **School Supply Kit, from Sharpie:** includes highlighters, pencils, pens, erasers, and more

GLUE AND GLUE STICKS

Kindergarten Classroom Supply Pack, from Crayola: includes 100 sheets of art paper, facial tissue, glue, crayons, water colors, markers, scissors, eraser, pencil case, 6 pencils, glue stick, and hand sanitizer

First and Second Grade Classroom Supply Pack, from Crayola: includes 2 folders, 100 sheets of art paper, 2 spiral notebooks, 200 pages of lined paper, facial tissue, composition book, 2 pens, crayons, colored pencils, washable markers, index cards, scissors, highlighter, eraser, pencil case, pencils, sharpener, glue stick, ruler, and hand sanitizer

Third Through Fifth Grade Classroom Supply Pack, from Crayola: includes 3 folders, 50 sheets of art paper, spiral notebook, 200 sheets of lined paper, composition book, 4 pens, crayons, colored pencils, washable markers, index cards, facial tissue, scissors, eraser, highlighter, pencil case, 6 pencils, sharpener, glue stick, ruler, and hand sanitizer

PENCIL GRIPS

These facilitate the correct grip for writing.

   The Pencil Grip Original Universal Ergonomic Writing Aid for
      Righties and Lefties, 6 Count, Assorted Colors
   The Pencil Grip Bumpy Grip Ergonomic Writing Aid
   The Classics 12-Pack Triangle Pencil Grip

BACKPACKS

Before shopping for a backpack, sit down with your child and plan all the different things your child will need for their day. Then anticipate when each thing will be needed. This will help you select the perfect backpack—with all the right pockets, nooks, and crannies. The backpacks below are recommended for their quality, sturdiness, and kid appeal.

   Jartop Elite Backpack
   School Uniform Backpack
   ClassMate TechPack Backpack

ClassMate Wheeled Backpack

L.L. Bean Deluxe Backpack

Deluxe Plus Book Pack

JanSport Right Pack Backpack

Rolling Deluxe Book Pack

Mini Berkeley Backpack

Youth Recon Squash Backpack

Chapter 2:
6:30 to 7:00 PM:
The Power of the Dinner (Half) Hour

Cookbooks for Nutritious, Easy Weekday Dinners

The Healthy Meal Prep Cookbook: Easy and Wholesome Meals to Cook, Prep, Grab and Go, by Toby Amidor

Make It Easy: 120 Mix-and-Match Recipes to Cook from Scratch, by Stacie Billis

Weeknight Paleo: 100+ Easy and Delicious Family-Friendly Meals, by Julie and Charles Mayfield

The Weeknight Dinner Cookbook: Simple Family-Friendly Recipes for Everyday Home Cooking by Mary Younkin

The School Year Survival Cookbook: Healthy Recipes and Sanity-Saving Strategies for Every Family and Every Meal (Even Snacks), by Laura Keough and Ceri Mash

Let's Cook French, A Family Cookbook: Cuisinons Francais, Un livre pour toute la famille, by Claudine Pepin

The Pollan Family Table: The Best Recipes and Kitchen Wisdom for Delicious, Healthy Family Meals, by Corki Pollan and Lori Pollan

It's All Easy: Delicious Weekday Recipes for the Super-Busy Home Cook, by Gwyneth Paltrow

Cookbooks for Small Families

Healthy Cookbook for Two: 175 Simple, Delicious Recipes to Enjoy Cooking for Two, by Rockridge Press

One Pan, Two Plates: More Than 70 Complete Weeknight Meals for Two, by Carly Snyder

Meal Planners and Shopping Lists

APPS

Shopkick

Food.com

GroceryIQ

PAPER BASED

Everyday Meal Planner with Perforated Shopping List and Tear off Sheets from Rifle Paper, available at riflepaperco.com and anthropologie.com

Bloom daily planners Weekly Meal Planning Pad with Magnets—Tear Off Meal Planner with Perforated, Tear-Off Shopping List, 6-inches by 9 inches

Educational Placemats

These placemats do double-duty: they protect the table while also offering valuable educational information.

MAP SKILLS

UNCLEWU United States Map-Educational Kids Placemats

Painless Learning Map of USA Placemat

Painless Learning Laminated Educational Placemats for Kids: USA Map, Asia Map, Africa Map, US State Flags with Capitals

Naanle Education Educational Placemat, Set of 6, Animal Map of the World

USA Map Memory Game and Activity Paper Placemats— Learn the States and Capitals on 25 Fun Double-Sided Worksheets

Melissa & Doug the United States Write-a-Mat Placemat

MATH PRACTICE

Melissa & Doug Math Skills Placemat Set—Addition, Subtraction, Multiplication, and Division

HANDWRITING PRACTICE

Melissa & Doug Alphabet and Numbers Placemats (Set of 3 Double-Sided Mats) with 5 Wipe-Off Crayons

Place Settings and Table Manners

Patch Products Inc. Blunders Manner Mats

Tot Talk Table Setting & Etiquette Educational Placemat for Kids, Washable and Long-Lasting

Table Manners

A good sense of humor is essential to teaching table manners. The resources below help add fun and light-heartedness to etiquette instruction.

Good Manners Flash Cards

Dinner with Olivia, by Emily Sollinger (book)

Dude, That's Rude! (Get Some Manners), by Pamela Espeland and Elizabeth Verdick (book)

Table Manners, by Chris Raschka and Vladimir Radunsky (book)

For Grown-Ups

Charleston Academy of Domestic Pursuits: A Handbook of Etiquette with Recipes, by Suzanne Pollak and Lee Manigault

Saying Grace

Christian Brands Large Wooden 2¼-inch Diameter Christian Mealtime Prayers Prayer Cube
Saying Grace: Blessings for the Family Table (book)
The Grateful Table: Blessings, Prayers and Graces (book)

Conversation Starters

These resources can be a part of the table setting and support lively dinner-time conversations.

Conversation Starters, available at www.thefamilydinnerproject .org
Conversation Starters for Kids—Questions for Kids for Family Dinner Discussions, available at Etsy
Conversation Cubes from FlagHouse
The Art of Children's Conversation, from Play Therapy Supply

Chapter 3:
7:00 to 7:30 PM: The Homework Hustle

For homework supplies, see the list in Chapter 1. For nights when your child has little to no homework, these activities will keep them engaged in learning while they play.

Academic Enrichment

STEM (SCIENCE, TECHNOLOGY, ENGINEERING AND MATH)

Engino Discovering Stem: Levers, Linkages & Structures Building Kit

Engino Discovering STEM Newton's Laws Inertia,
   Momentum, Kinetic & Potential Energy Construction Kit
National Geographic Mega Construction Engineering Set—
   Build 35 Unique Motorized Models: Helicopters, Cars,
   Animals and More—STEM Learning
Thames & Kosmos Barbie Crystal Geology Science Kit
Scientific Explorer: My First Science Kit
Scientific Explorer: Magic Science for Wizards Only Kit
SmartLab Toys Ultimate Secret Formula Lab
STEM at Play Soap Making Kit
Science X®: CSI Crime Scene Investigation
Scientific Explorer Crime Catchers Spy Science Kit

Gardening

Creativity for Kids Enchanted Fairy Garden Craft Kit—
Fairy Crafts for Kids
Children Flower Garden Kit—comes with organic flower
seeds, coloring planter case, and markers by Seeds of
Adventure
Nature's Blossom Grow 4 Herbal Tea Plants from Seed—
indoor herb garden growing kit with organic mint seeds,
catnip seeds, lemon balm, and chamomile, complete starter
set with soil, pots, labels, and guide
Nature's Blossom Fruit Growing Kit—the beginner's set to
grow four types of berries from seed: raspberries,
blueberries, goji berry, and blackberries; contains planting
pots, soil, and gardening guide
**Planters' Choice Organic Herb Growing Kit + Herb
Grinder**—complete kit to easily grow four herbs from
seed—basil, cilantro, chives, and parsley—with
comprehensive guide

Construction Kits

K'NEX 70 Model Building Set
Made by Me Build & Paint Your Own Wooden Cars, by
  Horizon Group USA

Archaeology Kits

Thames and Kosmos Classic Science Archaeology: Pyramid

Engineering Kits

Thames & Kosmos Kids First Automobile Engineer
LEGO City Arctic Ice Crawler 60033 Building Toy

Robotics

Wonder Workshop Dash Robots
LEGO Boost Creative Toolbox 17101 Building and Coding Kit
Snap Circuits Jr. SC-100 Electronics Discovery Kit

Math Enrichment

Bedtime Math series by Laura Overdeck and Jim Paillot
  (stories with word problems)
Great Estimations, by Bruce Goldstone (photos with math
  estimations)

Tinkering

Tinkerlab: A Hands-On Guide for Little Inventors, by Rochelle
  Doorley

Cooking

Kid Chef: Healthy Recipes and Culinary Skills for the New Cook in the Kitchen, by Melina Hammer

My First Baking Book: 50 Recipes for Kids to Make and Eat, by Becky Johnson

Visual Arts

Art Lab for Kids: 52 Creative Adventures in Drawing, Painting, Printmaking, and Mixed Media, by Susan Schwake

Art for Kids Comic Strips: Create Your Own Comic Strips from Start to Finish, by Art Roche

Sculpture

Play-Doh Modeling Compound 10-Pack or 24-Pack Case of Colors

Play-Doh Royal Carriage Featuring Disney Princess Cinderella

Play-Doh Kitchen Creations Spinning Treats Mixer

Play-Doh Soft Pack

Cool Sand

Adventure

Unbored: The Essential Field Guide to Serious Fun, by Elizabeth Larsen and Joshua Glenn

Jump Rope

Anna Banana: 101 Jump Rope Rhymes, by Joanna Cole

String Games

Cat's Cradle Book Kit by Anne Akers Johnson (Klutz)

Handclapping Rhymes

Miss Mary Mack and Other Children's Street Rhymes, by Joanna
  Cole

Card Games

These traditional games build memory, hand-eye coordination, patience, impulse control, and concentration.

> Uno
> Go Fish
> Concentration
> Hearts
> Solitaire

Other Puzzle Games

Sudoku
Hangman
SainSmart Jr. 40-Piece CB-23 Wooden Tangram Jigsaw Tetris
    Puzzle Toy
A Broader View 55-Piece Kids' Puzzle of the USA
Ravensburger Puzzles: See Inside Puzzles and 3-D Puzzles

Board Games

These games encourage a wide range of skill development, including turn taking, losing with grace, strategy, concentration, and
memory.

Trivial Pursuit Family Edition
Chess (exercises both parts of your brain and develops impulse
    control, memory, planning and judgment)
Checkers

Scrabble or Scrabble Jr.
Monopoly or Monopoly Jr.
The Classic Game of Jumanji
Clue
Carcassone
Hot Potato Jr.
Battleship
Stratego
Scotland Yard

Mad Libs

Mad Libs is a tried-and-true fun way to help children master parts of speech while creating absurd stories that they delight in sharing.

FOR CHILDREN AGED FIVE TO EIGHT

Super Silly Mad Libs Junior by Roger Price
Animals, Animals, Animals! Mad Libs Junior by Jennifer Franz
    and Leonard Stern
Sports Star Mad Libs Junior by Roger Price
School Rules! Mad Libs Junior by Leonard Stern

FOR CHILDREN AGED EIGHT TO TWELVE

Sleepover Party Mad Libs by Roger Price and Leonard Stern
Dog Ate My Mad Libs by Mad Libs
Goofy Mad Libs by by Roger Price and Leonard Stern
Mad Scientist Mad Libs by Mad Libs
Best of Mad Libs by Roger Price and Leonard Stern

Flash Cards

Flash cards get a bad rap, but they can be valuable aids in helping students memorize number facts, sight words, and other basic knowledge.

School Zone Reading Flash Card 4-Pack
Alphaprints Wipe Clean Flash Cards Numbers
Carson Dellosa CD-734007 Spectrum Flash Cards
    Subtraction
Addition Flash Cards Learning Numbers Game Thinking Skills
    Baby Toddler

KIDS NEW

Learning Playground Flash Cards, Multiplication
Spectrum Multiplication Flash Cards

Mazes

Mazes offer visual problem-solving that builds persistence.

From Here to There: A Book of Mazes to Wander and Explore by
    Sean Jackson
A-MAZE-ING Animals: 50 Mazes for Kids by Jos Wos
National Geographic Maze Adventures by Graham White

Coloring Books

These are wonderful for soothing an anxious child.

MoMA Color Coloring Book by Museum of Modern Art
I Absolutely Must Do Coloring Now by Lauren Child
Star Wars Doodle Activity Book by Ameet Studio
The National Parks Coloring Book by Sophie Tivona

The Usborne Book of Drawing, Doodling and Coloring by
    Fiona Watt and Erica Harrison

Creative Writing

Any notebook will do for most young writers, but the resources
below can help prime the pump.

Write Your Own Book (DK)
Write Your Own Adventure Stories (DK)

Chapter 4:
7:30 to 8:00 PM: Bed, Bath, and Beyond

Bath Toys

BATH TIME IMAGINATIVE PLAY

Meadow Kids Dress Up Bath Time Stickers
B. Toys Fish and Splish
IKEA: Smakryp 3-piece bath toy
Munchkin Tea and Cupcake Baby Bath Toy Set
Fisher-Price Shimmer and Shine Swing and Splash Genie Boat
Disney Princess Petite Toddler Ariel & Sisters Gift Set
Simba ABC 4-piece Bathing Ducks
Toysmith Wind-Up Submarine
ALEX Barber in the Tub
Hot Wheels® Tub Tracks Water Park Playset
Green Toys Ferry Boat with Mini Cars Bathtub Toy
Green Toys Seaplane
BathBlocks Floating Castle in Gift Box

BATH TIME MUSIC MAKING

ALEX Rub a Dub Water Flutes
ALEX Toys Rub a Dub Water Xylophone

BATH TIME MAP MAKING

ALEX Toys Bath USA Map in the Tub
ALEX Toys Bath World Map in the Tub

BATH TIME HAND-EYE COORDINATION

Skip Hop ZOO Bath Time Basketball-Dog
3 Bees & Me Bath Toy Basketball Hoop and Balls

BATH TIME CONSTRUCTION

Edushape Floating Blocks
Boon PIPES Building Bath Toy Set
BathBlocks: Floating Ball Run & Water Fall Set

BATH TIME VISUAL ARTS

Crayola Bathtub Crayons 9 Pack
Crayola Bathtub Fingerpaint Soap Fun
Crayola Bathtub Paint Brush Pens
ALEX Toys Rub a Dub Bath Writers

Book Time

Every child deserves a bookshelf filled with irresistible books in a wide range of genres. From pictures books to chapter books, reference books to mysteries, biographies to fairy tales, this list contains the very best books for children between the ages of five and twelve. They all make for excellent read-alouds.

And don't forget to check out the excellent audiobooks for children that appear further down in this list.

PICTURE BOOKS

Amelia Bedelia series, by Peggy Parrish
Blueberries for Sal, by Robert Mc Closkey

Make Way for Ducklings, by Robert Mc Closkey

Brave Irene, by William Steig

Sylvester and the Magic Pebble, by William Steig

Corduroy, by Don Freeman

Deep in the Sahara, by Kelly Cunnane

Don't Let the Pigeon Drive the Bus!, by Mo Willems

Goodnight Moon, by Margaret Wise Brown

Harold and the Purple Crayon, by Crockett Johnson

If I Had A Triceratops by George O'Connor

Little Bear, by Else Holmelund Minarik

Olivia, by Ian Falconer

Owl Moon, by Jane Yolen

Stellaluna, by Janell Cannon

The Cat in the Hat, by Dr. Seuss

The Lorax, by Dr. Seuss

The Frog and Toad collection, by Arnold Lobel

The Gingerbread Man, by Karen Schmidt

The Little Engine That Could, by Watty Piper

The Real Mother Goose, by Blanche Fisher Wright

The Red Balloon, by Albert Lamorisse

The Snowy Day, by Ezra Jack Keats

The Tale of Peter Rabbit, by Beatrix Potter

The True Story of the Three Little Pigs!, by Jon Scieszka

The Velveteen Rabbit, by Margery Williams

The Very Hungry Caterpillar, by Eric Carle

The Story of Ferdinand, by Munro Leaf

Tuesday, by David Wiesner

Where the Wild Things Are, by Maurice Sendak

The Story of Ruby Bridges, by Robert Cole

Malala's Magic Pencil, by Malala Yousafzai

FAIRY TALES, FOLK TALES, FABLES, AND LEGENDS

Animal Fables from Aesop, by Barbara McClintock

Arctic Aesop's Fables, by Susi Gregg Fowler

An Illustrated Treasury of Grimm's Fairy Tales: Cinderella, Sleeping Beauty, Hansel and Gretel and many more classic stories

An Illustrated Treasury of Hans Christian Andersen's Fairy Tales: The Little Mermaid, Thumbelina, the Princess and the Pea and many more classic stories

Bread and Jam for Frances, by Russell Hoban

Cinderella, or the Little Glass Slipper, by Marcia Brown

Classic Storybook Fables, by Scott Gustafson

Classic Bedtime Stories, by Scott Gustafson

D'Auliaires' Book of Norwegian Folktales, by Ingri and Edgar Parin D'Aulaire

Fables, by Arnold Lobel

Hansel and Gretel by Holly Hobbie

Jack and the Beanstalk, by Paul Galdone

John Henry: An American Legend, by Ezra Jack Keats

Johnny Appleseed: The Legend and the Truth, by Jane Yolen and Jim Burke

Little Critter series: Jack and the Beanstalk, Little Red Riding Hood, Hansel and Gretel and more

Little Red Riding Hood, by Trina Schart Hyman

LonPoPo, by Ed Young and B.D. Wong

Merlin and the Making of the King, by Margaret Hodges and Trina Schart Hyman

Miss Nelson Is Missing!, by Harry G. Allard and James Marshall

Not One Damsel in Distress, by Jane Yolen

Persephone, by Sally Pomme Clayton and Virginia Lee

Rapunzel, by Paul O. Zelinsky

Rumpelstiltskin, by Paul O. Zelinsky

Saint George and the Dragon, by Margaret Hodges and Trina Schart Hyman

The Sleeping Beauty, by Trina Schart Hyman

Strega Nona by Eric Carle

Stone Soup, by Marcia Brown

The Classic Treasury of Aesop's Fables, illustrated by Don Daily

The Golden Book of Fairy Tales

The Kitchen Knight: A Tale of King Arthur, by Margarte Hodges

The Three Little Pigs, by James Marshall

The Ugly Duckling, illustrated by Jerry Pinckney

Tikki Tikki Tembo, by Arlene Mosel

Swan Lake, as told by Margot Fonteyn

Yeh-Shen: A Cinderella Story from China, by Ai-Ling Louie

Saint George and the Dragon, by Margaret Hodges

MYTHS

D'Aulaires' Book of Greek Myths, by Ingri and Edgar Parin D'Aulaire

D'Aulaires' Book of Norse Myths, by Ingri and Edgar Parin D'Aulaire

The Gods and Goddesses of Olympus, by Aliki

The Mighty 12: Superheroes of Greek Myths, by Charles Smith

Greek Myths and Legends, by Cheryl Evans

Mythology, by Edith Hamilton

Norse Mythology, by Neil Gaiman

CHAPTER BOOKS FOR READERS IN KINDERGARTEN TO GRADE TWO

Clara Lee and the Apple Pie Dream, by Jenny Han

Dory Gantasmagory, by Abby Hanlon

Magic School Bus Chapter Book Series

Magic Treehouse Series, by Mary Pope Osborne

Time Warp Trio, by Jon Scieszka

Nate the Great, by Marjorie W. Sharmat

Fantastic Mr. Fox, by Roald Dahl

A Bear Called Paddington, by Michael Bond

CHAPTER BOOKS FOR READERS IN GRADE THREE TO GRADE FIVE

The Bolds, by Julian Clary

The Hundred Dresses, by Eleanor Estes

All of a Kind Family, by Sydney Taylor

Detectives in Togas, by Henry Winterfeld

The War That Saved My Life, by Kimberly Brubaker Bradley

Serafina's Promise, by Ann E. Burg

Ben and Me: An Astonishing Life of Benjamin Franklin by His Good Mouse Amos, by Robert Lawson

Phoebe the Spy, by Judith Griffin

CHAPTER BOOKS FOR READERS IN GRADES FOUR TO GRADE SIX

The Doorman's Repose, by Chris Raschka

Freaky Friday, by Mary Rodgers

Kira-Kira, by Cynthia Kadohata

Dragonwings, by Laurence Yep

Inside Out and Back Again, by Thanhha Lai

Heat, by Mike Lupica

Wonder, by R. J. Pallicio

Artemis Fowl, by Eoin Colfer

The Star of Kazan, by Eva Ibbotson

The Last Boy at St Edith's, by Lee Gjertsen Malone

The Stars Beneath Our Feet, by David Barclay Moore

Bronze and Sunflower, by Cao Wenxuan

Hatchet series, by Gary Paulson

Maniac Magee, by Jerry Spinelli

HISTORICAL FICTION

Out of the Dust, by Karen Hesse

The Devil's Arithmetic, by Jane Yolen

Catherine, Called Birdy, by Karen Cushman

A Diamond in the Desert, by Kathryn Fitzmaurice

Letters from a Slave Girl: The Story of Harriet Jacobs,
    by Mary E. Lyons

The Witch of Blackbird Pond, by Elizabeth George Speare

Esperanza Rising, by Pam Munoz Ryan

Fever 1793, by Laurie Halse Anderson

The Man Who Was Poe, by Avi

Copper Sun, by Sharon Draper

The True Confessions of Charlotte Doyle, by Avi

The Watsons Go to Birmingham, by Christopher Paul Curtis

A Single Shard, by Linda Sue Park

Nectar in a Sieve, by Kamala Markandaya Taylor

A Proud Taste for Scarlet and Minever, by E. L. Konigsburg

Letters from Rifka, by Karen Hesse

SCIENCE FICTION

These books are appropriate for fifth- and sixth-grade readers who
are strong readers.

A Wrinkle in Time, by Madeleine L'Engle

Brain Jack, by Brian Falkner

The City of Ember, by Jeanne DuPrau

The War of the Worlds, by H. G. Wells

FANTASY

Artemis Fowl, by Eoin Colfer

Ella Enchanted, by Gail Carson Levine

Eragon, by Christopher Paolini

Harry Potter series, by J. K. Rowling
Princess Academy series, by Shannon Hale
The Golden Compass, by Philip Pullman
The Never-Ending Story, by Michael Ende
The Phantom Tollbooth, by Norton Juster and Jules Feiffer
Tuck Everlasting, by Natalie Babbitt

CLASSICS

Adventures of Robin Hood, by Roger Lancelyn Green
Alice in Wonderland, by Lewis Carroll
Anne of Green Gables, by Lucy Maud Montgomery
Charlie and the Chocolate Factory, by Roald Dahl
Charlotte's Web, by E. B. White
Danny, Champion of the World, by Roald Dahl
James and the Giant Peach, by Roald Dahl
Little House on the Prairie series, by Laura Ingalls Wilder
Little Women, by Louisa May Alcott
Mary Poppins, by P. L. Travers
Peter Pan, by J. M. Barrie
Pippi Longstocking, by Astrid Lindgren
Sherlock Holmes: The Red-Headed League, by Arthur Conan Doyle
Stuart Little, by E. B. White
The Adventures of Robin Hood, by Howard Pyle
The Lion, the Witch and the Wardrobe, by C. S. Lewis
The Prince and the Pauper, by Mark Twain
The Secret Garden, by Frances Hodgson Burnett
The Story of King Arthur, by Howard Pyle
The Trumpeter of Krakow, by Eric. P. Kyle
The Trumpet of the Swan, by E.B. White
Treasure Island, by Robert Louis Stevenson
White Fang, by Jack London

MYSTERY AND ADVENTURE

A Series of Unfortunate Events, by Lemony Snicket
Chasing Vermeer, by Blue Balliett
Harriet the Spy, by Louise Fitzhugh
Holes, by Louis Sachar
The Eleventh Hour, by Graeme Base
The Invention of Hugo Cabret, by Brian Selznick
The Mysterious Benedict Society, by Trenton Lee Stewart
Theodore Boone, Kid Lawyer, by John Grisham
The Screaming Staircase, by Jonathan Stroud
The Westing Game, by Ellen Raskin

GRAPHIC NOVELS

Amulet, by Kazu Kibuishi
Comics Squad: Recess!, edited by Jennifer L. Holm, Matthew Holm, and Jarrett J. Krosoczka
Coraline, by Neil Gaiman
El Deafo, by Cece Bell and David Lasky
Fairy Tale Comics: Classic Tales Told by Extraordinary Cartoonists, edited by Chris Duffy
Hidden: A Child's Story of the Holocaust, by Loic Dauvillier and Greg Salsedo
Lost in NYC: A Subway Adventure, by Nadja Spiegelman, illustrated by Sergio Garcia Sanchez
Olympians: Zeus: King of the Gods, by George O'Connor
Smile, by Raina Telgemeier
Theseus and the Minotaur: A Toon Graphic, by Yvan Pommaux and Richard Kutner
Tintin, by Herge

BIOGRAPHIES FOR YOUNG READERS (KINDERGARTEN THROUGH THIRD GRADE)

Abe Lincoln Remembers, by Ann Turner

Abraham Lincoln, by Ingri D'Aulaire

Ada Byron Lovelace and the Thinking Machine, by Laurie Wallmark

Benjamin Franklin, by Ingri D'Aulaire

George Washington, by Ingri D'Aulaire

Grace Hopper: Queen of Computer Code, by Laurie Wallmark

Henry's Freedom Box, by Ellen Levine

My Dream of Martin Luther King, by Faith Ringgold

Pocahontas, by Ingri D'Aulaire

Rosa, by Nikki Giovanni

The Girl Who Thought in Pictures: The Story of Dr. Temple Grandin, by Julia Finley Mosca

Time for Kids biographies series (subjects include Benjamin Franklin, Thomas Edison, Clara Barton, Alexander Graham Bell, Jesse Owens, Jackie Robinson, Abigail Adams, Theodore Roosevelt, Eleanor Roosevelt, and more)

BIOGRAPHIES FOR OLDER ELEMENTARY READERS (THIRD GRADE THROUGH SIXTH GRADE)

And Then What Happened, Paul Revere?, by Jean Fritz

Childhood of Famous Americans biography series (including Harriet Tubman, Lou Gehrig, Crispus Attucks, Betsy Ross, Helen Keller, Daniel Boone, Coretta Scott King, Sacagawea, Langston Hughes, Frederick Douglass, Jackie Robinson, Rosa Parks, Jesse Owens, Christopher Reeve, Arthur Ashe, Ray Charles, and more)

Christopher Columbus, by Peter Roop and Connie Roop

I Am Malala: How One Girl Stood Up for Education and Changed the World, adapted by Patricia McCormick for younger readers

If You Were There in 1492, by Barbara Brenner

Through My Eyes, by Ruby Bridges

Wanted Dead or Alive: The True Story of Harriet Tubman, by Ann McGovern

NONFICTION

Aaron and Alexander: The Most Famous Duel in American History, by Don Brown

A Child's Introduction to African American History, by Jabari Asim

For the Right to Learn: Mala Yousafzai's Story, by Rebecca Langdon-George, illustrated by Jenna Bock

Going Solo, by Roald Dahl

Gravity, by Jason Chin

Let It Shine: Stories of Black Women Freedom Fighters, by Andrea Davis Pinkney

Marching for Freedom, by Elizabeth Partridge

Mr. Ferris and His Wheel, by Kathryn Gibbs Davis

Rebel with a Cause: The Daring Adventure of a Girl Spy of the American Revolution, by Dicey Langston

Sadako and the Thousand Paper Cranes, by Eleanor Coerr

The Endless Steppe: Growing Up in Siberia, by Esther Hautzig

The Family Romanov, by Candace Fleming

Warriors Don't Cry, by Melba Pattillo Beals

We Are the Ship: The Story of Negro League Baseball, by Kadir Nelson and Dion Graham

Wheels of Change: How Women Rode the Bicycle to Freedom, by Sue Macy

Words Set Me Free: The Story of Young Frederick Douglass, by Lesa Cline-Ransome

POETRY

A Book of Nonsense, by Edward Lear

A Child's Garden of Verses, by Robert Louis Stevenson

A Child's Book of Poems, by Gyo Fujikawa
A Poke in the I, by Christopher Raschka
Brown Girl Dreaming, by Jacqueline Woodson
Old Possum's Book of Cats, by T. S. Eliot
Poems to Learn by Heart, edited by Caroline Kennedy
The Giving Tree, by Shel Silverstein

REFERENCE

Dorling Kindersley Children's Illustrated Encyclopedia
Guinness World Records
National Geographic Student World Atlas
Scholastic Children's Dictionary
Scholastic Student Thesaurus
Smithsonian Children's Encyclopedia of American History
World Almanac for Kids

BIBLE

Bible Stories for Children, by Johannes Wyss
The Complete Illustrated Children's Bible, by Janice Emmerson

Audiobooks

Audiobooks are the great, overlooked medium of American childhood. These recorded books invite some of the greatest actors of all time into your home to read to you and your child. Audiobooks are perfect for nights when you simply prefer to listen than to read aloud. You and your child can always silently read along in your book while listening to the recording. These are fantastic when your child is home with a cold to play in the background while they recuperate.

Audiobooks are also ideal for times when you and your children are cooking or working on a crafts project. Listening to the story while tinkering with a project feels relaxing and engaging all at once. Another great thing about audiobooks? The best ones just get better the more times you hear them. Audible is a treasure trove of audio recordings for children.

Here are some audiobooks that you and your child won't want to miss.

DR. SEUSS

Green Eggs and Ham, narrated by Jason Alexander
The Cat in the Hat, narrated by Kelsey Grammer
Oh, the Places You'll Go!, narrated by John Lithgow
The Lorax, narrated by Ted Danson

POEMS, SONGS, AND LULLABIES

Julie Andrews' Collection of Poems, Songs and Lullabies
Julie Andrews' Treasury for All Seasons
Old Possum's Book of Practical Cats, narrated by Miranda Richardson
Ted Hughes Poems for Children, narrated by Juliet Stevenson, Ted
    Hughes, and more

CLASSIC STORIES ENACTED BY A FULL CAST OF ACTING LEGENDS

Winnie the Pooh and the House at Pooh Corner, featuring Judi
    Dench, Stephen Fry, and a full cast
The Moffats, narrated by Cynthia Bishop and cast

CHAPTER BOOKS WITH OUTSTANDING NARRATORS

Sarah, Plain and Tall, by Patricia MacLachlan, narrated by Glenn
    Close
The Hobbit, by J. R. R. Tolkien, narrated by Rob Inglis
A Series of Unfortunate Events, by Lemony Snicket, narrated by
    Tim Curry
Anne of Green Gables, by L. M. Montgomery, narrated by Rachel
    McAdams

Matilda, by Roald Dahl, narrated by Kate Winslet

The Roald Dahl Audio Collection, narrated by the author

D'Aulaire's Book of Greek Myths, narrated by Paul Newman, Sidney Poitier, and others

The Lion, the Witch and the Wardrobe, narrated by Michael York

Peter Pan, narrated by Jim Dale

A Bear Called Paddington, narrated by Stephen Fry

Boy, by Roald Dahl, narrated by Dan Stevens

The Watsons Go to Birmingham, narrated by LeVar Burton

Nancy Drew series, narrated by Laura Linney

Maniac Magee, narrated by S. Epatha Markeson

Children's Journals

Any notebook will do for a journal, but your child may benefit from the inspiration in these journals. And as an added bonus, they become precious keepsakes.

All About Marvelous Me!: A Draw and Write Journal, by Becky J. Radtke

I Am Grateful: Kids Gratitude Journal/Gratitude Notebook for Children: With Daily Prompts for Writing and Blank Pages for Coloring, by Cute Notebooks

Me: A Compendium: A Fill-In Journal for Kids, by Wee Society

All About Me Lock & Key Diary, by Peaceable Kingdom Press

Bedtime Prayers

PLC 1½-Inch Wood Children's Kids Sunday School Church Bedtime Prayers Cube

Lucado Treasury of Bedtime Prayers

Words to Dream On: Bedtime Bible Stories and Prayers

Prayer for a Child, by Rachel Field and Elizabeth Orton Jones

Lullabies

Why do we abandon lullabies once babies become toddlers? Lullabies can still work their magic on older children as they drift off to sleep.

Brahms' Lullaby
"Lullabye (Goodnight, my Angel)," by Billy Joel
"Clair De Lune"
"Moon River"
"Once Upon a Dream"

Night-Lights

These adorable night lights will be a friendly presence in your child's room after lights out.

Aloka Robot Night Light, from Aloka Sleepy Nights
Primary Night Light, from The Land of Nod
Teepee Night Light, from The Land of Nod
Campsite Night Light, from the Land of Nod

Chapter 5:
8:00 PM: You Time

Here are some resources for the parent after the children have gone to bed.

Cleaning and Preparing for the Next Day

BOOKS ON TIDYING UP

The Life-Changing Magic of Tidying Up, by Marie Kondo
The Complete Book of Clean: Tips and Techniques for Your Home, by Toni Hammersley
The Complete Book of Home Organization, by Toni Hammersley

Meal Containers
(Lunch Boxes for Children and Adults
as well as Leftovers)

Yumbox

ECOlunchbox: Three-in-One Stainless Steel Food Container
   Set

MERCIER Leak-Proof Premium Bento Lunch Box with
   Cutlery Set

APPS FOR PLANNING AND CALENDARING

Timepage

Evernote

Any.do

Outlook

Trello

APPS FOR VISUALIZATION AND GOAL SETTING

Amazon Echo: Night Routine, Morning Routine

Google Home

Strides

Way of Life

GoalsonTrack

A Tracker

Taking Stock

JOURNALS AND HAPPINESS PLANNERS

Journaling before bed can help us take stock of the day and plan
thoughtfully for the future. Although any notebook will do, the following resources can help.

JOURNALS FOR RECORDING MEMORIES OF ONE'S CHILDREN

My Quotable Kid: A Parents' Journal of Unforgettable Quotes, by Chronicle Books

Stories for My Child (Guided Journal): A Mother's Memory Journal, by Samantha Hahn

JOURNALS FOR SELF-EXPLORATION

Start Where You Are: A Journal for Self-Exploration, by Meera Lee Patel

JOURNALS FOR IMPROVING ONE'S MOOD

The Simple Abundance Journal of Gratitude, by Sarah Ban Breahnach

The One-Minute Gratitude Journal, by Brenda Nathan

The Happiness 100-Day Planner, by Brand Mentalist

The Five Minute Journal: A Happier You in 5 Minutes a Day, by Intelligent Reading

ONLINE READING CLUBS

When you can't get to a reading club in person, these online reading clubs can motivate you to read and feel connected to a community of readers.

Reese Witherspoon's Book Club: Follow Reese Witherspoon's Book Club on Instagram and reply to the posts to join the discussion.

Oprah's Book Club 2.0: Join the discussion on the Oprah's Book Club Goodreads page, or post your opinion of the book on Twitter and Instagram (hashtag #oprahsbookclub).

Andrew Luck Book Club: Luck posts two recommendations on his website—a children's book and a book for adults. Read the featured book and post your thoughts on Twitter, Instagram, or Facebook (hashtag #albookclub).

Relaxing

Everything you need to hygge: Hygge doesn't just happen. It needs to be cultivated. Candles, music, slippers, and warm drinks are all non-negotiable. You may want to create a hygge kit so you can hygge whenever the mood strikes.

CANDLES

Candles are essential to Hygge. Whether you prefer flameless or scented candles, this list has you covered.

French Lavender Candle, from Williams Sonoma
Pottery Barn Pillar Candles
Pottery Barn Premium Flickering Flameless Wax Taper Candle
Pottery Barn Premium Flickering Flameless Wax Candle
Pottery Barn Luminara Remote Control
Diptyque Scented Candles, various scents
Voluspa Maison Candle, various scents

MUSIC

Any warm, happy, relaxing music will do. Here are a few suggestions.

Swedish Traditional Folk Songs, by Elina Järventaus Johansson
Downton Abbey Christmas Album
Bridge Over Troubled Water, by Simon & Garfunkel
Nat King Cole and Me, by Gregory Porter

BLANKET

Lilac Coast: Lambswool Pattern Blanket with Fringes

L.L. Bean: Hudson's Bay Point Blanket

L.L. Bean: Maine-Made Cotton Blanket

Eileen Fisher Waves Cashmere Throw

Pottery Barn Faux Sheepskin Throw

HOT COCOA

What could be cozier on a cold winter's evening than a cup of hot chocolate? Just avoid having it right before bed, as it can keep you up.

MarieBelle Aztec Hot Chocolate

Taza Mexicano Discs Cacao Puro

Jacques Torres Wicked Hot Chocolate

Jacques Torres Classic Hot Chocolate

HYGGE-ISH MOVIES

Any movie that makes you feel good and is life affirming is ideal for hygge. Here are some suggestions.

It's a Wonderful Life

Little Women

Love Actually

Breakfast at Tiffany's

The Notebook

SLIPPERS

H&M Cashmere Slippers

Vineyard Vines Women's Cashmere Ballet Slippers

L.L. Bean Women's Wicked Good Sheepskin Shearling Lined
    Moccasin Slippers

UGG Dakota Slippers

MEDITATION AND MINDFULNESS APPS

Calm (Android/iOs)
Headspace (Android/iOs)
Buddhify (Android/iOs)
The Mindfulness App (Android/iOs)
Aura (Android/iOs)
Oak (Android/iOs)
Mindbliss (Android/iOs)

Preparing to Sleep

TEA

These teas encourage relaxation and are perfect in the hours before bed.

Tea Luxe Sweet Chamomile Mint Organic
Tea Luxe Chamomile Medley
Tranquil Dream Herbal Tea
Celestial Seasonings Wellness Tea, Sleepytime Extra
Traditional Medicinals Herbal Nighty Night Tea
Bigelow Benefits Herbal Tea, chamomile and lavender

Music Before Bed

For music that increases sleepiness, explore playlists such as the Fall Asleep playlist at Google Play. Also check out:

SOUNDSCAPES

Noisli (app for creating customized relaxing soundscapes)
Weightless (an eight-minute track by Marconi Union that was made in collaboration with sound therapists. It was specifically composed to decrease stress, blood pressure, and resting heart rates.)

WHITE NOISE

White Noise app (good for children and parents)

Epsom Salts and Bubble Baths

Sleep Salts Organic Lavender Essential Oil Epsom and Dead
  Sea Bath Salts

Dr. Teal's Pure Epsom Salt Soaking Solution Soothe and Sleep
  with Lavender

Honest Bubble Bath (Ultra Calming)

Episencial Peaceful Bubbles

EYE MASKS

Eye masks are a great alternative to blackout curtains for blocking
out all light and encouraging deep sleep.

Slipsilk Pure Silk Sleep Mask

Alaska Bear Natural Silk Sleep Mask, available at Amazon

Lilac Dot Lavender Sleep Mask, from Nordstrom

REM Sleep Mask-Midnight Blue, from Napgear

Acknowledgments

Thank you to the wonderful principals, teachers, parents, and students I have been so lucky to work with and learn from through the years. I particularly want to acknowledge the contributions of Ms. Napoli and her fourth-grade class in the Bronx. These youngsters warmed my heart with their enthusiasm for this book, constantly asked if it was published "already," and gave advice on everything from the cover design to what constitutes good table manners. They even offered to write "blurbs" for the back cover copy; one of my favorites of which was, "If Ms. Miller had never been born, hugs would never have been invented." Testimonials don't get any better than that!

Sixth-grade teacher Constance Bedson inspired me with ideas about homework centers with her thoughtful use of task lamps and other interior design elements to create a warm and inviting atmosphere for her students in Brooklyn. Her equally brilliant colleague Rachel Amoako was a marvel at developing the intellectual and verbal capacities of her eleven-year-old students through Socratic dialogue. Their good example, and the examples of so many other educators I have had the privilege of working with, helped inform the practices in this book.

I was fortunate to work with many talented people on the book's production; from illustrator Tammy Want who produced the delightful illustrations that grace the book's pages to Lori Hobkirk at the Book Factory who beautifully managed the book's production, from Josephine Moore's outstanding copyediting to the lovely interior design by Cynthia Young.

My agent, Erika Storella at the Gernert Company, has championed this book from the proposal stage through to publication. Thank you, Erika, for all your support, enthusiasm, and guidance.

217

My amazing editor, Dan Ambrosio at Da Capo, was a delight to work with and helped shape the manuscript in innumerable ways. He was superbly assisted by Miriam Riad. Finally, I want to thank Da Capo's publisher John Radziewicz and vice president Lissa Warren for their vision and commitment to this book from its earliest stages.

Last but not least, I want to thank my family and friends for their support and encouragement. My son, Jasper, deserves the greatest thanks of all for giving me the joy of being his parent for the past twenty-five years; a job that happily never ends.

Notes

Preface

xiii   "The average American parent spends": A. R. Lauricella, D. P. Cingel, L. Beaudoin-Ryan, M. B. Robb, M. Saphir, and E. A. Wartella, "The Common Sense Census: Plugged-In Parents of Tweens and Teens 2016," Common Sense Media, www.commonsensemedia.org/research/the-common-sense-census -plugged-in-parents-of-tweens-and-teens-2016.

xiii   "Our concentration spans": Megan Willett, "A Study Says Teens Are Spending Nearly All Their Waking Hours Staring at Screens," *Business Insider*, May 26, 2016, http://www.businessinsider.com /teens-average-phone-screen-usage-2016-5.

xiv   "In 2018 the average American child": Victoria L. Dunckley, MD, "Gray Matters: Too Much Screen Time Damages the Brain," *Psychology Today*, February 27, 2014, https://www.psychology today.com/us/blog/mental-wealth/201402/gray-matters-too-much -screen-time-damages-the-brain.

xv   "We often set a time after": Aatif Sulleyman, "Bill Gates Limits His Children's Use of Technology," *The Independent*, April 21, 2017, https://www.independent.co.uk/life-style/gadgets-and-tech /news/bill-gates-children-no-mobile-phone-aged-14-microsoft -limit-technology-use-parenting-a7694526.html.

xv   "They haven't used it": Chris Weller, "Bill Gates and Steve Jobs Raised Their Kids Tech-Free—and It Should Have Been a Red Flag," *Business Insider*, January 10, 2018, http://www.business insider.com/screen-time-limits-bill-gates-steve-jobs-red-flag-2017-10.

xv   "Today a surprising number": Ibid.

xv   "Media products are designed": Amy Fleming, "Screen Time v Play Time: What Tech Leaders Won't Let Their Own Kids Do," *The Guardian*, May 23, 2015, https://www.theguardian.com /technology/2015/may/23/screen-time-v-play-time-what-tech -leaders-wont-let-their-own-kids-do.

Introduction

3   "According to the American Academy of Sleep Medicine":
     American Academy of Pediatriatrics, "American Academy of
     Pediatrics Supports Childhood Sleep Guidelines," June 13, 2016,
     https://www.aap.org/en-us/about-the-aap/aap-press-room/pages
     /American-Academy-of-Pediatrics-Supports-Childhood-Sleep
     -Guidelines.aspx.

3   "With adequate sleep, children enjoy": "Improve Your Memory
     with a Good Night's Sleep," n.d., https://sleepfoundation.org
     /sleep-news/improve-your-memory-good-nights-sleep.

4   "The blue light from screens": "Blue Light Has a Dark Side,"
     Harvard Health Publishing, December 30, 2017, https://www
     .health.harvard.edu/staying-healthy/blue-light-has-a-dark-side.

Chapter 1

12   "More than 90 percent of moms and dads": "Percentage of
     Parents with Children Under Age 13 Who Provided Various
     Forms of Warmth and Affection Every Day During the Past
     Month: 1997," ChildTrends, www.childtrends.org/wp-content
     /uploads/2013/04/52-Table-1.pdf.

12   "A hug lowers stress": Stacey Colino, "The Health Benefits of
     Hugging," *US News & World Report*, February 3, 2016.

12   "Hugging promotes the release": Sheldon Cohen, Denise Janicki-
     Deverts, Ronald B. Turner, and William J. Doyle, "Does Hugging
     Provide Stress-Buffering Social Support? A Study of
     Susceptibility to Upper Respiratory Infection and Illness,"
     Psychological Science 26, no. 2 (February 2015): 135–147.

18   "Working in silence is the optimal": Daniel A. Gross "This Is Your
     Brain on Silence," *Nautilus*, August 21, 2014, http://nautil.us
     /issue/16/nothingness/this-is-your-brain-on-silence.

23   "The executive function refers": "Executive Function & Self-
     Regulation, n.d., https://developingchild.harvard.edu/science
     /key-concepts/executive-function/.

23 "And here's something all parents should know": Ibid.

31 "In New York City, a recent study": "Restaurant Grading in New York City at 18 Months," n.d., New York: New York City Health.

Chapter 2

39 "Children raised in families": Julie R. Thomson, "The Very Real Psychological Benefits of Cooking for Other People," October 17, 2017, https://www.huffingtonpost.com/entry/benefits-of-cooking-for-others_us_5967858ae4b0a0c6f1e67a15.

40 "Incredibly, only 11 percent": "Recent Handwashing Study Shows Gap Between Knowing and Doing," n.d., https://www.asm.org/index.php/component/content/article/114-unknown/unknown/6360-recent-handwashing-study-shows-gap-between-knowing-and-doing.

41 "If your hands are wet or damp": "Handwashing: Clean Hands Save Lives," March 7, 2016, https://www.cdc.gov/handwashing/index.html.

46 "People who regularly express": "Giving Thanks Can Make You Happier," Harvard Health Publishing, n.d., https://www.health.harvard.edu/healthbeat/giving-thanks-can-make-you-happier.

52 "Eating in front of a television": "6 Reasons You Should Not Watch TV While Eating," July 13, 2016, http://thescienceofeating.com/2016/07/13/6-reasons-you-should-not-watch-tv-while-eating/.

52 "Just having a phone or device": Jill Suttie, "How Smartphones Are Killing Conversation," December 7, 2015, https://greatergood.berkeley.edu/article/item/how_smartphones_are_killing_conversation.

54 "Because decontextualized talk": Meredith L. Rowe, "Decontextualized Language Input and Preschoolers' Vocabulary Development," 2013, https://dash.harvard.edu/bitstream/handle/1/13041200/Rowe%202013.pdf?sequence=1.

Chapter 3

71 "Silence increases blood flow": Daniel A. Gross, "This Is Your Brain on Silence," *Nautilus*, August 21, 2014, http://nautil.us /issue/16/nothingness/this-is-your-brain-on-silence.

72 "A 2013 study of brain structure": John Rosca, "True Silence Creates New Brain Cells, Improves Memory," July 13, 2016, https://www.natureworldnews.com/articles/25132/20160713 /true-silence-creates-new-brain-cells-improves-memory.htm.

77 "Often a well-intentioned parent": A. Pawlowski, "Why You Shouldn't Help Your Kids with Their Homework," *Today*, April 28, 2014, https://www.today.com/parents/why-you-shouldnt-help-your -kids-their-homework-1D79558306.

81 "The idea that adults can focus": Cynthia Kubu and Andre Machado, "The Science Is Clear: Why Multitasking Doesn't Work," May 31, 2017, https://health.clevelandclinic.org/science -clear-multitasking-doesnt-work/.

85 "The National Education Association and National PTA": Justin Worland, "Too Much Homework: Children Receive 3 Times Recommended Amount," *Time*, August 12, 2015, http://time .com/3994039/recommended-homework-load-stress/.

91 "As every organization guru": Mike Stieb, "3 Things to Do Before Bed That Will Energize You the Next Day," *Fortune*, May 18, 2017, http://fortune.com/2017/05/17/leadership-career-advice -morning-bedtime-routine-sleep-exercise/.

94 "Organization plays a critical": Jill M. Gambill, Laurlee A. Moss, and Christie D. Vescogni, "The Impact of Study Skills and Organizational Methods on Student Achievement," Saint Xavier University, May 2008, https://files.eric.ed.gov/fulltext /ED501312.pdf.

99 "The minimal guidelines on the table": "Research Spotlight on Homework," n.d., http://www.nea.org/tools/16938.htm.

Chapter 4

101 "Bedtime rituals make it easier": "Perfecting Your Child's Bedtime Routine," n.d., https://sleepfoundation.org/sleep -news/perfecting-your-childs-bedtime-routine.

107 "According to the American Association of Pediatrics": "Dental Health & Hygiene for Young Children," October 14, 2015, https://www.healthychildren.org/English/healthy-living/oral-health /Pages/Teething-and-Dental-Hygiene.aspx.

108 "Children should brush for a full": "Toothbrushing Tips for Young Children," November 21, 2015, https://www.healthychildren.org /English/healthy-living/oral-health/Pages/Toothbrushing-Tips-for -Young-Children.aspx.

116 "Children, Sigmund Freud said": Raymond G. McInnis, "Dr. Benajamin Spock's Baby and Child Care: Origins, Impact, Sources," *Reference Services Review* 13, no. 4, 9–15.

125 "The body and mind love ritual": Alva Noë, "The Habitual Brain: How Routine Action and Thought Are the Structure of Life," NPR, September 24, 2010, https://www.npr.org/sections/13.7 /2010/09/22/130051236/the-habitual-brain.

127 "As a result, the hormone melatonin": Alina Bradford, "How Blue LEDs Affect Sleep," February 26, 2016, https://www.livescience .com/53874-blue-light-sleep.html.

128 "While there are individual differences": "Touch," 2018, https://sleepfoundation.org/bedroom/touch.php.

Chapter 5

135 "Most adults need anywhere from seven": "How Much Sleep Do We Really Need," n.d., https://sleepfoundation.org/excessives leepiness/content/how-much-sleep-do-we-really-need-0.

137 "I've written some of my best stuff": Bob Doerschuk, "10 Things We Learned When Billy Joel Interviewed Don Henley," *Rolling Stone*, September 21, 2015, https://www.rollingstone.com/music /news/9-things-we-learned-from-billy-joels-interview-with-don -henley-20150921.

137 "The best time for planning a book": Alison Abbey, "Agatha Christie Quotes to Celebrate the Author's 125th Birthday," *Parade*, September 14, 2015, https://parade.com/422725 /alison-abbey/15-agatha-christie-quotes-to-celebrate-the -authors-125th-birthday/.

137 "Housework burns about 165 calories": John P. Buckley et al., "The Sedentary Office," *British Journal of Sports Medicine* 49, October 16, 2015.

138 "Ancestors could have told us": Anthony Rivas, "Happiness Comes from New Experiences, Not Material Objects, Even When They Haven't Happened Yet," *Medical Daily*, September 6, 2014, https://www.medicaldaily.com/happiness-comes-new-experiences -not-material-objects-even-when-they-havent-happened -yet-301650.

142 "Travel is one of the experiences": Ben Groundwater, "Science Proves that Travel Is the Secret to Happiness," *Traveller*, September 25, 2017, http://www.traveller.com.au/ science-proves-that-travel-is-the-secret-to-happiness-gix3mw.

146 "Having a genuine support system": Zoe E. Taylor et al., "Parenting Practices and Perceived Social Support: Longitudinal Relations with the Social Competence of Mexican-Origin Children," *Journal of Latina/o Psychology* 3, no. 4, 2015, 193–208.

148 "The spirit of hygge is a celebration": Marie Tourell Søderberg, *Hygge: The Danish Art of Hygge*, New York: Penguin, 2016.

149 "The most important contributor to our psychological": Simon Sinclair, "A Very British Type of Hygge," *The Telegraph*, July 4, 2017, https://www.telegraph.co.uk/property/home-improvement -tips/hygge-safe-and-secure-at-home/.

152 "Adding Epsom salts to your bath": Susan Patterson, "9 Irresistible Reasons You Should Have an Epsom Salt Bath Today," July 10, 2017, http://www.naturallivingideas.com /epsom-salt-bath/.

152 "There is some evidence that playing video games": Grant Bailey, "Playing Video Games Is a Key Strategy for Coping with Stress,

Study Finds," *The Independent*, February 9, 2018, https://www
.independent.co.uk/life-style/video-games-stress-playing-strategy
-key-gamers-study-a8202541.html.

153   "Writing in a journal helps relax": Maud Purcell, "The Health
Benefits of Journaling," March 22, 2018, https://psychcentral
.com/lib/the-health-benefits-of-journaling/.

153   "Using a journal to express gratitude": Oprah, "An Exclusive Look
at Oprah's Journals," n.d., http://www.oprah.com/spirit/oprahs
-private-journals-diary-excerpts.

154   "Playing relaxing music": Andy Chiles, "Reading Can Help
Reduce Stress, According to University of Sussex Research,"
The Argus, March 30, 2009, http://www.theargus.co.uk/news
/4245076.Reading_can_help_reduce_stress__according_to
_University_of_Sussex_research/.

154   "Reading fiction is the best stressbuster": Ibid.

155   "According to a study at Yale University": "Book Up for a Longer
Life: Readers Die Later Study Finds," *The Guardian*, August 8,
2016, https://www.theguardian.com/books/2016/aug/08/book-up
-for-a-longer-life-readers-die-later-study-finds.

155   "Reading strengthens the brain": Christopher Bergland, "Reading
Fiction Improves Brain Connectivity and Function," *Psychology
Today*, January 4, 2014, https://www.psychologytoday.com/us/blog
/the-athletes-way/201401/reading-fiction-improves-brain
-connectivity-and-function.

155   "Because reading a novel forces": David Comer Kidd et al.,
"Reading Literary Fiction Improves Theory of Mind," *Science*
342, no. 6156 (Oct 18, 2013): 377–380.

Chapter 6

158   "Structure helps us steady": "Health Benefits of Having a
Routine," n.d., http://www.nmbreakthroughs.org/daily-health
/health-benefits-of-having-a-routine.

160   "Overachievers from Barack Obama to": Jacquelyn Smith, "Steve
Jobs Always Dressed Exactly the Same. Here's Who Else Does,"

Forbes, November 12, 2012, https://www.forbes.com/sites
/jacquelynsmith/2012/10/05/steve-jobs-always-dressed-exactly
-the-same-heres-who-else-does/#75eb52c65f53.

160   "I'm trying to pare down": Ibid.

160   "I really want to clear my life": Avery Hartmans, "Mark
Zuckerberg Just Showed Off His First New Outfit in Years—It'll
Cost You $1,000 to Steal His New Look," *Business Insider*, May 1,
2018, http://www.businessinsider.com/mark-zuckerberg-gray
-t-shirt-uniform-update-blue-sweater-f8-2018-2018-5.

162   "Each day Spanish parents spend": Alysse ElHage, "Parents'
Shared Time in the U.S., Spain, and France," February 8, 2017,
https://ifstudies.org/blog/parents-shared-time-in-the-u-s-spain-and
-france.

162   "French parents enjoy forty minutes": Ibid.

163   "Nothing has a stronger influence": Hyde Schools, "Parents:
Are They Making the Grade?" October 13, 2009, http://www
.hyde.edu/blog/2009/10/13/parents-are-they-making-the-grade/.

165   "The authoritative parenting style is": Emily Hughes, "Types of
Parenting Styles and How to Identify Yours," December 10, 2013,
https://my.vanderbilt.edu/developmentalpsychologyblog/2013/12
/types-of-parenting-styles-and-how-to-identify-yours/.

166   "Psychologists speculate that the worse": Judith Woods, "Have
Sweden's Permissive Parents Given Birth to a Generation of
Monsters?" *The Telegraph*, February 13, 2014, https://www
.telegraph.co.uk/women/mother-tongue/10636279/Have-Swedens
-permissive-parents-given-birth-to-a-generation-of-monsters.html.

168   "As many as 46 percent": Katie Hurley, "How Parental Stress
Negatively Affects Kids," April 21, 2017, https://health.usnews
.com/wellness/for-parents/articles/2017-04-21/
how-parental-stress-negatively-affects-kids.

168   "Studies have shown that parental": Ibid.

Conclusion

171 "A landmark Harvard study tracked": Liz Mineo, "Good Genes Are Nice, But Joy Is Better," *Harvard Gazette*, April 11, 2017, https://news.harvard.edu/gazette/story/2017/04/over-nearly-80 -years-harvard-study-has-been-showing-how-to-live-a-healthy -and-happy-life/.

173 "Furthermore, American married": Elizabeth Warren, "What Happened to the Middle Class?" *CNN*, May 1, 2014, https:// www.cnn.com/2014/05/01/opinion/warren-middle-class/index .html.

176 "Studies of people who live into": Tamekia Reece, "10 Habits of People Who've Lived to Be 100," *Prevention*, December 24, 2016, https://www.prevention.com/life/ g20498364/10-habits-of-people-whove-lived-to-be-100/.

177 "As the landmark seventy-five-year": Robert Waldinger, "What Makes a Good Life? Lessons from the Longest Study on Happiness," n.d., https://en.tiny.ted.com/talks/robert_waldinger _what_makes_a_good_life_lessons_from_the_longest_study_on _happiness.

179 "An enormous source of resentment": Wendy Klein, Carolina Izquierdo, and Thomas N. Bradbury, "The Difference Between a Happy Marriage and Miserable One: Chores," *The Atlantic*, March 1, 2013, https://www.theatlantic.com/sexes/ archive/2013/03/ the-difference-between-a-happy-marriage-and-miserable-one- chores/273615/.

Index